THE BIBLE IN THE
ASHES OF SOCIAL CHAOS

THE
BIBLE
in the Ashes of Social Chaos

An Introduction to Problematic Texts

LEWIS BROGDON

Foreword by Chris Caldwell
Afterword by Beau Brown

 CASCADE *Books* · Eugene, Oregon

THE BIBLE IN THE ASHES OF SOCIAL CHAOS
An Introduction to Problematic Texts

Cascade Books
An Imprint of Wipf and Stock Publishers
199 W. 8th Ave., Suite 3
Eugene, OR 97401

www.wipfandstock.com

PAPERBACK ISBN: 978-1-6667-4988-5
HARDCOVER ISBN: 978-1-6667-4989-2
EBOOK ISBN: 978-1-6667-4990-8

Cataloguing-in-Publication data:

Names: Brogdon, Lewis. | Foreword by Chris Caldwell. | Afterword by
Beau Brown.

Title: The Bible in the ashes of social chaos : an introduction to problematic texts / Lewis Brogdon.

Description: Eugene, OR: Cascade Books, 2023 | Includes bibliographical
references.

Identifiers: ISBN 978-1-6667-4988-5 (paperback) | ISBN 978-1-6667-4989-2
(hardcover) | ISBN 978-1-6667-4990-8 (ebook)

Subjects: LCSH: Bible—Black interpretations. | Bible—Criticism, interpre-
tation, etc. | African Americans—Religion. | Bible—Reading.

Classification: BS511.3 B76 2023 (print) | BS511.3 (ebook)

Contents

Foreword by Chris Caldwell vii

PART ONE: *Getting Honest about the Bible*

1. The Bible—Important but not Read 3
2. The Bible—A Different Kind of Text to Interpret 15
3. Problematic Texts in the Bible 34
4. Interpreting Problematic Texts 55

PART TWO: *From the Text to Our Context*

5. The Bible and Incarnational Truth 77
6. Collateral Damage and the Bible 86
7. Reimagining the Bible's Relevance for Today 100

Afterword by Beau Brown 113
Bibliography 117

Foreword

CHURCHES TOO OFTEN EXCEL at spotting specks in the eyes of the passersby. Lewis Brogdon instead wants churches to spend less time looking out windows and more time looking in mirrors. Churches too often play the blame game; Lewis Brogdon prefers we shoulder responsibility and take action. If, for example, someone is honest enough to admit struggling with an unnerving passage of Scripture, churches often feel the remedy is for the person to get themselves in line with the text and set aside any reservations they might have. The text is the perfect master, and we are to be its unquestioning servants. Brogdon's method is instead more like Jacob wrestling with the angel. Brogdon does not deny the authority of the text, but he works at a hermeneutic that respects the authority of the text while at the same time not surrendering the autonomy of the reader.

This wrestling style of interpretation cuts across the grain of the text, rather than with it. Some texts don't require this kind of interpretation. When reading the twenty-third Psalm, we don't need to cut against the grain; we just need to slip into the stream of the psalm. But what to do when we read one of the texts Brogdon notes, Ps 137:9: "Happy is the one who seizes your infants and dashes them against the rocks (NIV)"? These sorts of passages demand we read against the grain of the text. The question then becomes, how do we read against the grain of text yet respect the authority of the Bible that contains them? This is the worthy subject of Brogdon's book.

A unique contribution of this book is how it turns questions of biblical interpretation in the direction of declining enthusiasm for church. Karl Barth famously observed one must "do theology with the Bible in one hand, and the newspaper in the other." Barth's admonition is not to forget the newspaper. Brogdon is aligned with Barth, but he reverses the idea. When it comes to the problems ailing churches, we need not to forget the issue of how we read the Bible. There are excellent books out there on the "Nones" (those with no church connection) and the "Dones" (those who severed church connections). But most of them, in my opinion, are more "newspaper" than "Bible." They do an excellent job of looking at cultural currents and mining sociological data, which is important. But in certain respects, they lean toward looking out the window at the weather outside the church, where Brogdon here challenges us to look at the climate inside our sanctuaries. With specific emphasis on biblical interpretation, he asks what we might do to be more honest about the Bible and some of the parts which trouble us—and which, frankly, keep some people from coming to church at all.

Brogdon has a pattern of wrestling with difficult biblical issues facing churches. His early work, *Hope on the Brink: Understanding the Emergence of Nihilism in Black America*, challenged us to consider problems causing people to abandon the hope offered by faith. In his more recent work, *A Companion to Philemon*, he builds on the work of others who have tried to rehabilitate the interpretation of a book long seen as supporting slavery. All biblical scholars seek to "open up the text," but what I like about Brogdon's work is that the text he opens serves as a drawbridge into the church. We who love churches see the Bible as a warm invitation. Truth be told, especially for African Americans, many parts of the Bible feel less like a bridge to faith and more like a wall. Brick by brick, book by book, Brogdon's careful and compelling scholarship is tearing down walls between people and churches, and, to his credit, Brogdon realizes these walls have not sprung simply from the imaginations of the skeptics but have foundations in our careless interpretations and lazy habits. This book, and his scholarship, are invitations to travel a "stony road" toward a deeper faith and truer church.

Dr. Chris Caldwell, Chair of the Department of Religious Studies, Simmons College of Kentucky, Louisville Kentucky

Part One

Getting Honest about the Bible

Chapter One

The Bible—Important but not Read

THE BELIEF THAT THE Bible is the word of God, the sacred text of the Christian religion, and the most influential book in Western society is held by millions of people. The Bible is deeply revered by Roman Catholic, Eastern Orthodox, Fundamentalist, Evangelical, Mainline, Pentecostal, Charismatic, and nondenominational Christians. It is valued for its inspiring stories, critically studied as a religious text by scholars, taught and preached from as an authoritative guide in matters of faith by bishops, priests, pastors, and ministers, and its characters, images, and ideas are utilized in innumerable ways from art, music, literature, law, public policy, and even televisionand movies.

Yet, in spite of the Bible's widespread importance, its contents are ignored by many people, even those who preach and teach it. The truth is American Christians do not read the Bible as much they used to, and their knowledge of the basic contents is embarrassingly low. In recent decades, the Bible has become the most important, but unread, book in America. In the age of mega churches, televangelism, and more Bible college, university, and seminary trained ministers than the U.S. church has had in any era in our brief history, Americans read the Bible less and know less of its contents than any time in our history.

A growing number of religious scholars, researchers, and congregational pastors are witnessing this firsthand. An article

3

written in 2000 and published in *The Washington Post* discussed the continuing importance yet growing neglect of the Bible by Christians.

> About 92 percent of Americans own at least one, and the average household has three. Two-thirds say it holds answers to the basic questions of life . . . It is the Bible, also known as "the Good Book," and it remains as the world's all-time bestseller. It is also widely and frequently hailed as the underpinning of American values . . . [but] Americans are showing themselves to be remarkably ignorant of Bible basics . . . The Bible, it seems, is the book that everyone wants to read, but few do.[1]

Further evidence was given in the book *Religious Literacy* by Stephen Prothero. In it, he chronicled a major paradox about the Bible and religion in America when he argued that Americans are both deeply religious yet profoundly ignorant. In America, strong and deep feelings about the importance and centrality of one's faith are common and widespread. Yet, deep feelings and beliefs are held by people who are ignorant about the contents of the very book they believe is sacred and which is the basis of those beliefs. He found that many American Christians cannot name the Ten Commandments or the four Gospels. Prothero listed results of surveys done on biblical literacy and the findings are revealing.

- Bible reading has declined since the 1980s.

- Bible knowledge is at a record low.

- Only half of American adults surveyed could name even one of the four Gospels, and most could not name the first book of the Bible.

- A majority of Americans wrongly believe that the Bible says that Jesus was born in Jerusalem.

- A majority of Americans do not know that Jonah is a book in the Bible.[2]

1. Gibson, "We Revere the Bible . . . We Don't Read It."
2. Prothero, *Religious Literacy*, 38–39.

4

Prothero's work reveals how biblically illiterate Americans have become during a time when religion is so central to our lives, our communities, and the nation. Although important, popular, and widely referenced, it is clear that the Bible is not being read with care and understanding.

There is a deeper problem here. Prothero's work reveals that the real problem is the large numbers of Christians who are disconnected from the disciplines of careful reading and studying the Bible. I have witnessed some of what Prothero documents. I accepted a call into the ministry at the young age of nineteen while a freshman in college. I remember when I announced my call to the ministry at my home church, Miracle Mount Carmel Holiness Church of God in Kimball, West Virginia. They were so happy and excited about what God was doing in my life. I recall my uncle, Melvin Jeter, coming to visit us, and he asked me if I had a Bible. I was proud to tell him that I had recently purchased my first Bible. He said, "Good, if you are going to be a preacher you better know the Bible." I spent the summer of 1992 reading through the Bible and the next twenty-five years teaching the Bible. In fact, in 2010, I became a scholar of the Bible when I graduated from Regent University with a PhD. I wrote my dissertation on Paul's brief letter to Philemon. I have done all this because of my formation in the Holiness Church, a church that expected that anyone preaching or teaching should be knowledgeable of the Bible. What I have come to realize is that this expectation is not reality for many others. I have come to realize that people in church do not read the Bible very much.

I pastored congregations in four states—Virginia, West Virginia, Kentucky, and Ohio. I have also preached and taught seminars in many churches all over the United States, and I know hundreds of pastors. I have seen firsthand the waning commitment to reading the Bible by congregants. They opt for what I like to call "devotional reading." This form of reading consists of reading a passage out of the Psalms or Proverbs or reading a passage out of a popular devotional that closes with a verse for the day. While inspirational and meaningful for a lot of people, this is really not reading the Bible, and I have serious reservations whether or not it can deepen faith. They read the Bible devotionally because it is important to them, but there is no escaping the irony that it is not important enough to read in detail and with care. I often observed that the number of congregants willing to read and study the Bible was lower than the number who came to worship on Sundays to hear the weekly sermon. Those who attended Bible study or a Christian education class of some kind, often called Sunday school, had a better understanding of the Bible, but I was always surprised by the fact that even they really had not read much of the Bible. Often their participation in class replaced personal reading and studying. Many based their knowledge of the Bible on the interpretations of Scripture heard in sermons. Sometimes their knowledge was based on popular clichés and sayings they had heard from their favorite preachers. As a Sunday school teacher, I cannot count the times I have asked the simple question, "Where does it say that in the Bible?" and the response was a dumbfounded look and "I don't know." I will not even comment on the two decades of conversations I have had with clergy about the Bible. Too many study the Bible for sermon purposes and teach Bible study lessons but do not consistently read the Bible. It is a surprising and discouraging fact.

I have also worked in both a theological seminary and a university department of religion. I have taught a number of exegetical courses on individual books in the New Testament as well as introductory surveys of both the Hebrew Bible/Old Testament and the New Testament. In my years of teaching, it is apparent that the knowledge of the Bible among those studying for ministry is marginal when they enter school. Test scores of entrance exams assessing their knowledge of the Bible are low, which shows the lack of reading and studying occurring in congregations. Moreover, I have been disappointed to see young people, who are already bright stars in the church and preaching everywhere, failing basic exams on the Bible and earning low grades in biblical content courses. In those Bible content courses, I have assigned entire books or large portions of the Bible to be read along with the course texts. I am always surprised that students will not read the biblical text but opt, instead, for reading the course text by a prominent scholar. Let me remind you that these are the students who are currently leading churches and will do so for years to come. They refused to sit down and carefully read the Bible in content courses preparing them for ministry and religious leadership.

In a real sense, the importance of the Bible is a distraction because people, including people of faith, are not reading it in the first place. Too many churches put too much energy into maintaining the Bible's importance and function as an authoritative text in the church and society and put too little energy into reading the Bible. I do not believe that the Bible needs to be venerated more than it is read.

The Question Why

Why do the people who believe the Bible is important fail and sometimes even refuse to read it? In my work as both a biblical scholar and minister of thirty years, I have identified three reasons why some people do not read the Bible. First, people read less of the Bible because it is *time-consuming*. Considering the volume of material in the Bible (66 books) and the busy lives people lead today, some Christians choose to substitute active personal reading and study for passive listening to sermons. The rationale is, "Since I hear sermons based on Bible texts every time I attend a worship service, and sermons teach things about the Bible, I choose not to read the Bible myself." A second reason people fail to read the Bible is that they *struggle to understand* some parts of it. For example, some translations of the Bible, like the King James Version, have words or ideas that may be hard to understand (e.g., pay tithe of mint, anise, and cumin in Matt 23; baptism for the dead 1 Cor 15:29). Because of any one or all of these reasons, some people become discouraged from reading and studying the Bible. I am not going to devote additional discussion to this here because I believe these are obstacles pastors and other resources can address.

There is also a third reason. Some people intentionally choose not to read the Bible, and some even refuse to read the Bible. They do so because they are *turned off by statements* which I like to call, "problematic texts" in the Bible. In a sense, for some readers, certain parts of the Bible cancel out the relevance and broader meaning of the whole of the Bible. Our cultural obsession with those "problematic" parts is one of the perennial issues of our time as it often determines how a person views the Bible and whether they will read it.

Though widely popular and revered, the Bible is a controversial religious text. It says controversial things that some people are not aware of, things that people would agree with, and things people would rather avoid or strongly disagree with (commands such as kill the men, women and children 1 Sam 15:3; women keep quiet in church 1 Cor 14:34; slaves obey your masters Ephesians 6:5). At times, this causes some people to disregard or avoid the Bible altogether. In fact, I have found that problematic texts are a real concern for a growing number of thoughtful believers. Sadly, too many pastors ignore them or become defensive, and they refuse to have honest and critical conversations about these texts. Our communities are filled with people with doubts, concerns, questions, and criticisms about things stated in the Bible. Look at the following examples from two online articles.

> I recall as a child thinking it was a tad unfair that God struck down someone who was carrying his Ark with a bolt of lightning (2 Samuel 6:1–7 and 1 Chronicles 13:9–12). Surely his tripping and falling was an accident not punishable by death? Something else that bares noting, is that if you believe God has written our lives and fates beforehand (it's also called Predestination), did Judas Iscariot have any choice in his betrayal of Jesus? Wasn't he predestined to be damned? Because some man had to be Jesus' betrayer, one feels it is a bit much allocating this damnable act to any person. Here's a list of bible verses that make one wonder just what sort of God Christians give their lives to in sincere patronage to what they call 'Holy' . . . And speaking of lying, the Bible ends with

one. It calls its message 'the good news' and concludes, "I am coming soon." Wrong on the 'soon' bit, and unless we've missed something, no one has come. But I get it, if 2000 years pass, soon after such a length of time must be VERY soon. If 10,000 years pass, soon must be very VERY soon.[3]

This second quote from Jeremy Myers makes the connection between certain texts and atheism in a compelling way.

I was recently having a discussion with an atheist who had grown up in a Christian family and had gone to church for the first twenty years of her life. But she became an atheist in her 20s. When I asked her why she became an atheist, she said, "I started reading the Bible." We Christians often tell people that if they would only read the Bible, they would come to see that God is real and that He loves them. We hear testimony after testimony about how drug addicts and hookers were considering suicide but somehow got a Bible and started reading it and ended up giving their life to Christ. I am not in any way denying such accounts or stories. But I think it is also time to admit that, while many people decided to follow Jesus as a result of reading the Bible, there are many others who turned away from God after reading the Bible. Part of this, I am convinced, is because we Christians have said that the entire Bible is the Word of God, but then we ignore, gloss over, conveniently forget, or are simply dishonest about some of the more troubling portions of Scripture. And there are many troubling portions of Scripture! (If you don't believe me, read this book: *Drunk with Blood*). I call these troubling texts "Atheist Maker Verses." They are verses that do not point people to God, but instead lead people away from Him.[4]

The world of the internet and social media is inundated with these types of articles and blog posts. The Myers articles had over one hundred comments from readers who sought to lend credence to the troubling verses in the Bible and their role in producing

3. "14 Most Abominable Bible Verses."
4. Myers, "11 Bible Verses That Turn Christians Into Atheists."

atheism, those who sought to defend the Bible, and those who tried to find a middle ground of some sort. It is a hot-button and highly controversial issue that interests people, and they need conversation partners.

People turning away from the Bible because they have questions about problematic texts is a real concern for me as both a minister and biblical scholar. Since I believe that reading and studying Scripture are vital parts of the life of faith, I have taken up the work of addressing obstacles that prevent this from happening. While there are clearer translations of the Bible and many resources explaining difficult words and ancient cultural practices, less attention is given to controversial or problematic texts, except by people sometimes bent on destroying instead of deepening faith.

I hope to provide a primer with three audiences in mind. First, I am writing for people in the church who are interested in thinking critically about this important book called the Bible and its relevance for life today. This is needed because so many have been told "what" the Bible is rather than being taught "how" to read and interpret it. Many are content with this approach and will simply classify this book as liberal and heretical theology. It is easier than wading pastorally and critically into issues of interpretation. However, I write this text for Christians willing to do this important work of reading the Bible thoughtfully, both for their own lives of faith and to prepare themselves for engaging people with honest questions. Throughout this book I am especially mindful of my siblings in African American churches. One of the greatest challenges I face as a Black scholar of the Bible is the widespread influence of fundamentalist theology. Many African American denominations subscribe to the doctrine of inerrancy and other beliefs adopted from the same theological traditions that fought to enslave and segregate them in previous eras. It is a grotesque irony to say the least.

I have directed two Black church studies programs and worked with hundreds of churches. I have found that African American churches are often resistant to the questioning and critical thinking I model here. What is so disappointing is that it is a betrayal of the genesis of the Black church as a corrective movement of white Christianity's gross misrepresentation of Christianity. Yet today, many Black congregations and its pastors do not give their leaders and congregants space to reimagine the Bible's relevance in new ways. Just as we see a growing number of religious "noncs" in mainline churches, there is a growing number of African American Christians in estranged relationships with their churches and denominations. Some of our estranged siblings feel that the church worships a book rather than God. Others reject the insistence on a static system of faith that holds to oppressive beliefs like the subordination of women, homophobia, God cursing non-tithers, God not caring for social justice, and dangerous forms of Black nationalism that encourage hatred of others.

Black churches need to give Black people space to grapple with hard questions and deepen their faith. This book along with Angela Parker's new book *If God Still Breathes Why Can't I?* are resources to support such important work.[5] Historically, churches have been safe spaces from racism where Black people crafted an identity not confined to racism's lies, violence, and systems. This history can make questioning faith appear to weaken a source of strength and meaning for a vulnerable community. Yet there is a different and healthier way to think about questioning faith. We should reframe questioning as a return to the faith that gave rise to slave religion and Black churches in the first place. Leaders in Black churches have work to do if we want a viable future; that work begins with an honest assessment of the devastating effects of fundamentalist theology on Black faith.

How did African American churches get so off track? Vincent Wimbush chronicled the emergence of fundamentalist thinking in *The Bible and African Americans: A Brief History*. In the 1940s and

5. Parker provides much-needed nuance and context to the doctrine of inerrancy. As inerrancy and infallibility are not terms found anywhere in the Bible, they are products of the minds of men, particularly white men. She argues that this doctrine is an expression of white supremacist authoritarianism and works to teach people how to move from bibliolatry to inspired biblical authority. *If God Still Breathes Why Can't I?*

50s, more African American denominations began to adopt beliefs that viewed the Bible as a "deracialized, depoliticized and universal guide to truth and salvation" and, more importantly, "that religious truth can now be claimed to have transcended historical experience."[6] This approach has significant implications for the living out of faith in a country defined by slavery and racism. Having Black preachers, Black meaning-makers interpreting the Bible in ways that ignore the particularities of the Black experience represents a significant departure from the preaching and interpretation of Scripture that enabled Black people to endure centuries of slavery. No matter how commendable the focus on soul salvation, personal piety, and worship may be, there is no escaping the devastating effect this will have on churches and people trying to make sense of a racialized world. This is why Wimbush is so critical of this development. It is tragic in that this form of interpretation led to "self-emptying, self-questioning and self-contempt; all experienced on a superficial level as a certain construct of piety."[7] In a sense, this theology in Black churches set the stage for a growing disconnect young and progressive African Americans experienced with Black churches. Two large and very influential grassroots racial justice movement in recent years—Black Lives Matter and the American Descendants of Slavery (ADOS)—arose in response to criminal justice and economic systems that often fail to address the material needs of African Americans. Both movements were not products of the Black church as Dr. King's Southern Christian Leadership Conference (SCLC) was in the fifties and sixties. They were also not led by heterosexual clergymen but instead by members of the diverse LGBTQI community, some of whom are committed Christians that interpret the Bible differently than traditional Black church denominations. A smaller yet significant development has been Black nationalist groups like the Hebrew Israelites. They have challenged traditional Black churches for its Eurocentrism, namely its worship of a white Jesus and its ignorance about Christianity's African roots. A significant component

6. Wimbush, *Bible and African Americans*, 69.

7. Wimbush, *Bible and African Americans*, 75.

of their challenge has been focused on texts in the Bible. From BLM to Hebrew Israelites, these movements are all signals of a crisis of identity for the Black church and the ways we approach the Bible.

However, Wimbush and others are a part of a growing discipline in the field of biblical studies called African American Biblical Interpretation (hereafter referred to as AABI). AABI is one of the newer streams in contemporary hermeneutics and has done much to help us assess the Bible's history in the hands of white Christians and to reimagine its relevance for the world today.[8] AABI explores the nature and task of a Black hermeneutical approach to Scripture. As a hermeneutical discipline, AABI examines the following subjects: (1) Black hermeneutical approaches to interpretation, which include the function of Scripture in the related disciplines of Black Theology, Black Preaching, African American worship, and its function in African American churches; (2) the African presence in Scripture or Afro-centric interpretation; (3) history of Black engagement with Scripture; (4) Womanist interpretations of Scripture; and (5) African American commentaries, translations, and study Bibles.

African Americans have engaged Scripture for over three hundred years. As such, one of the aims of Black religious scholarship is to identify the distinct features of the historical African American engagement with Scripture and to determine how these efforts have served to buttress every facet of the Black religious experience. This study will bring together two fundamental tasks for Black hermeneutics: correcting the Eurocentric bias that ignores our history with problematic texts,and examining the ways we interpret the Bible to speak specifically and meaningfully to our experiences. This is a major motivation behind this project.

---

8. AABI is a term utilized first by Cain Hope Felder in the text *Stony the Road We Trod*, and then by Michael J. Brown to describe African American or Black approaches to interpretation in *The Blackening of the Bible*. AABI is also called Afrocentric interpretation in Bailey, *Yet With a Steady Beat*; Floyd, *Black Biblical Studies or Hermeneutics in Black Church Studies*; and Black hermeneutics in Thiselton, *New Horizon's in Hermeneutics.*.

Second, I am writing this for first-year undergraduate students taking a course in Bible. I have taught "Introduction to the Bible" for years and always wanted a text that introduced the Bible and its interpretation in light of questions I raise here. I found young people were not concerned with old questions and traditional beliefs about the Bible. What made them sit up in class and lean into discussions were questions about texts on slavery, divorce, hell etc. I was always struck by the ways they grappled with texts marginalizing women or their gay friends. They would argue with the Bible on those points but not discard it. This book is a reflection of those engaging discussions with hopes it will serve as a resource for future students.

Third, I am writing for people who are struggling with their faith or those grappling with hard questions. I want to encourage them in their struggle. It is ok. God is not threatened because you have doubts or questions about things in the Bible. Any caring and honest reader should have questions. I believe there are insights in this book that will help you on your journey. I hope this primer serves as a tool to shift the Bible's use in modern culture from a weapon to minimize and marginalize people and shut down questions that could clarify, direct, and deepen faith. This book will model intellectual honesty and moral imagination in ways that provide paths back to faith and theologies that are different from those wedded to Eurocentric Christianity as it continues to collapse around us. While religious prognosticators herald the new age of atheism, I believe newer, healthier streams of Christian faith are on the horizon. God is doing a new thing that requires new thinking about the Bible.

As a primer, there will always be more that needs to be said, but my purpose is to introduce the issue and help readers understand the complexities involved in interpreting these texts. I will, however, reference texts that provide more depth and context for readers who want to take the next step in their study after completing this primer. I cannot think of a more pertinent faith issue than problematic texts in the Bible.

Chapter Two

The Bible—
A Different Kind of Text to Interpret

THE BIBLE IS A book, but it is not "just" a book. The Bible is a sacred text with a rich history and influence spanning centuries. The Bible was the first book ever put to the printing press. The man who first printed it, Johannes Gutenberg, was voted the most important man to have ever lived within the past one thousand years! Today, it is believed by many to be the most popular and widely read book in the world, with more than 100 million new copies produced every year, and it has been translated into every known language. One noted scholar summarized the significance of the Bible as follows:

> The influence of the Bible permeates every aspect of life in the 20th century Western world- laws, literature, art, music, architecture, morals, and religion. Many of the Bible's words and phrases are a part of our current speech and allusions to its stories are widely understood. It is a vital part of our total cultural heritage; indeed, many people would claim that it is, for a variety of reasons, the most important and influential collection of writings ever brought together and bound in a single volume. The Bible is a perennial best seller and has been

translated into more than a thousand different languages
and dialects.[1]

People have looked to the Bible for inspiration, guidance,
and hope in the darkest of times, especially for African Americans. Vincent Wimbush, a Black biblical scholar, explained that
the Bible functioned as a language world for Africans in America
who were first introduced to Scripture as enslaved people. They
learned to view and define themselves in biblical terms because
the Bible "quickly came to function as a language world, the store-
house of rhetorics, images, stories, that through a complex history
of engagements, helped establish African Americans as a circle of
biblical imaginary."[2] This idea of the Bible as a language world was
significant because it showed how important Scripture was in the
long process of fighting enslavement, and in defining them as people created by the God of the Bible called to be free. I say all that to
show that the Bible is a different kind of book, and when people of
faith open its pages and read what is written, they are reading this
text in a qualitatively different way than other texts are read.

Overview of the Bible

An important first step in interpreting problematic texts is to see
Scripture in its entirety. For example, the Protestant Bible, different in some ways from the Scriptures read by Roman Catholic
and Eastern Orthodox Christians, contains sixty-six books. This
means the Bible is not just a book, but a large multivolume book,
a point often ignored.

1. Hayes, *Introduction to the Bible*, 3.
2. Wimbush, *Bible and African Americans*, 3.

Chart 1: Books in the Protestant Bible

Old Testament

Genesis	Exodus	Leviticus
Numbers	Deuteronomy	Joshua
Judges	Ruth	1 Samuel
2 Samuel	1 Kings	2 Kings
1 Chronicles	2 Chronicles	Ezra
Nehemiah	Esther	Job
Psalms	Proverbs	Ecclesiastes
Song of Solomon	Isaiah	Jeremiah
Lamentations	Ezekiel	Daniel
Hosea	Joel	Amos
Obadiah	Jonah	Micah
Nahum	Habakkuk	Zephaniah
Haggai	Zechariah	Malachi

New Testament

Matthew	Mark	Luke
John	Acts	Romans
1 Corinthians	2 Corinthians	Galatians
Ephesians	Philippians	Colossians
1 Thessalonians	2 Thessalonians	1 Timothy
2 Timothy	Philemon	Hebrews
James	1 Peter	2 Peter
1 John	2 John	3 John
Jude	Revelation	

These writings are divided into two sections: Old and New Testaments. The Old Testament, also known as the Hebrew Bible, was originally written in Hebrew and Aramaic. The New Testament was written in Koine Greek. Both testaments were written by various authors over a span of centuries from the ancient Near East, Africa, and the Greco-Roman world. These writings, thirty-nine in the Old Testament and twenty-seven in the New Testament, cover events that begin with the creation of the world and end with the Day of Judgment and eternity. These writings also contain various genres such as narratives, proverbs, parables, letters, prophecies, and apocalyptic literature and was later canonized by Jews and Christians as authoritative writings that guide belief and teaching. There is a tremendous amount of material contained in this multivolume book.

- There are 929 chapters in the writings of the Old Testament and 260 chapters in the writings of the New Testament.

- Some writings in the Old Testament are very large—Genesis has 50 chapters, Exodus has 40 chapters, Job has 42 chapters, Isaiah has 66 chapters, Jeremiah has 52 chapters, and Ezekiel has 48 chapters.

- There are 23,145 verses in the Old Testament and 7,958 verses in the New Testament. That is a total of 31,103 verses. [Note: the exact numbers depend on the edition and translation of the Bible].

- There are over 613 commandments in the Old Testament.

- There are 150 psalms in the book of Psalms.

- There are 31 chapters of proverbs (wisdom sayings) in the Book of Proverbs with anywhere between twenty-five and thirty proverbs per chapter.

- There are over forty parables in the Gospels.

- Chapter 27 of Matthew contains 66 verses.

- There are as many as 1000 commandments in the writings of the New Testament.

I cannot stress enough the importance of recognizing the breadth of material. It is a major interpretive factor. How does one account for so much material in a single text? The attempt to systematize or organize this much material is very challenging and maybe impossible. So, instead of attempting to develop a system or theology that uses every single verse in the Bible, most Christians choose to select the more important parts, believing they represent the whole. However, they do not use everything, and we need to be honest about this.

Believing in Everything in the Bible but Not Using It

Many Christians believe that the Bible is inspired by God and an unparalleled source in matters of faith. Preachers will vehemently argue that all sixty-six books are the word of God. They will dogmatically claim that every book in the Bible points to Jesus Christ. However, their belief in the whole Bible does not mean they actually use everything in it. One reason they do not use everything in the Bible is because of the tremendous amount of material gathered into this single volume. Instead, most Christians who interpret the Bible today are selective in what they use. Some claim to read and use every verse in the Bible in their theological system, but they do not. I have heard more sermons than I can count and know that certain texts or parts of the Bible are ignored and not used. I have read hundreds of theological texts, commentaries, and monographs and have yet to find one that uses every single verse in the Bible. Theologians and scholars are selective with the passages they use to talk about God, faith, and life in this world. Christians in churches do the same thing. The truth is pastors in churches do not create comprehensive or exhaustive beliefs and theologies based on every verse in the Bible. The Christians in the pews are not even reading every verse in the Bible.

Why is this important? Because one of the first things I want my readers to understand is that being selective with the Bible does not mean you are disrespecting the Bible. Almost all Christians do it. This is important because problematic texts are sometimes omitted or avoided by people who believe such statements do not reflect the truth of God or are not central to the larger story the Bible portrays about God and humanity. In fact, a person being selective with the Bible by not ascribing value and authority to a problematic text is actually doing the same thing most devout Christians do. They are just doing it for different reasons. No one, and I mean no one, uses every part of the Bible in preaching, teaching, theology, etc. They identify parts that they believe reflect some important aspect of the message and use those while ignoring or not utilizing others. Let me give two very practical examples of this. First, examine these two texts. One Scripture is used to explain how salvation works and the other is ignored and not used in preaching and teaching, except for an occasional historical reference to practices in ancient Israel.

Chart 2: Sample Textual Comparison

Applicable Text	Non-Applicable Text
If you declare with your mouth, "Jesus is Lord," and believe in your heart that God raised him from the dead, you will be saved. For it is with your heart that you believe and are justified, and it is with your mouth that you profess your faith and are saved. (NIV)	If your offering is a fellowship offering, and you offer an animal from the herd, whether male or female, you are to present before the Lord an animal without defect. You are to lay your hand on the head of your offering and slaughter it at the entrance to the tent of meeting. Then Aaron's sons the priests shall splash the blood against the sides of the altar. (NIV)

We do this all the time. We choose to assign broader importance and application to texts which focus on salvation issues while glossing over passages which are rooted in Israel's history or texts advocating practices we no longer follow, like sacrificing animals to God. Second, there are hundreds of verses in the Bible that contain miscellaneous or what I call "filler" information. The verses are included in the Bible but are not particularly instructive in matters of faith. They do not offer instruction or make prohibitions of some kind. They just list names, places, or give context to a story.

Chart 3: Filler Verses

Bible Verse	Information Given (quoting KJV)
Gen 2:13	And the name of the second river is Gihon: the same is it that compasseth the whole land of Ethiopia.
Exod 6:17	The sons of Gershon; Libni, and Shimi, according to their families.
Num 1:12	Of Dan; Ahiezer the son of Ammishaddai
Deut 34:3	And the south, and the plain of the valley of Jericho, the city of palm trees, unto Zoar

These verses are important because they tie larger stories together but are not really given much thought by readers. In fact, these verses are ignored. These verses do not create disagreements or controversy, largely because they do not drive the narrative. Readers do not have to discard the entire Bible because select texts are not always applicable.

The practice of selecting, and I will add prioritizing, certain texts is more common than we believe. Let me explain how this works. To read, study, and apply in some way a book containing this much material requires a system of some kind. One has to identify, organize, and systematize teachings and stories in a way that results in a basic understanding of the theological message of the Bible and then to use this basic message to support and guide teaching in the church. Often churches have creeds, confessions, or statements of faith. They do not reflect every verse in the Bible but instead draw on select texts that are viewed in a normative and paradigmatic manner. The first creed of the church utilized this approach. It drew on the writings of the Old Testament and early Christian writings to frame a creed.

The Apostles' Creed

I believe in God, the Father almighty, creator of heaven and earth. I believe in Jesus Christ, his only Son, our Lord, who was conceived by the Holy Spirit and born of the virgin Mary. He suffered under Pontius Pilate, was crucified, died, and was buried; he descended to hell. The third day he rose again from the dead. He ascended to heaven and is seated at the right hand of God the Father almighty. From there he will come to judge the living and the dead. I believe in the Holy Spirit, the holy catholic church, the communion of saints, the forgiveness of sins, the resurrection of the body, and the life everlasting. Amen.

Sample Statement of Faith

- The Triune God as Father, Son, and Holy Spirit (Gen 1:26; Isa 6:8; Matt 28:18–20; 2 Cor 13:14)

- God as creator of the universe and humankind (Gen 1:1–31; John 1:1–3; Acts 17:24–26)

- The death of Jesus Christ for the sins of the world (John 3:16; Rom 3:21–26; 1 Pet 2:24)

- Salvation that is available for all through Jesus Christ by faith, repentance, confession and baptism (Rom 10:9–11; Acts 2:38; Eph 2:8; 1 Pet 3:21; Mark 16:15–16)

- The ministry of the Holy Spirit as comforter, teacher, intercessor, and source of gifts for ministry (John 14:16–16, 26; 1 John 2:27; Rom 8:26–27; 1 Cor 12:1–31)

- The truthfulness and authority of the Scriptures to guide believers in righteousness and matters of faith (2 Tim 3:16–17; 2 Pet 1:20–21)

- The church as God's elect, bride of Christ and agent of ministry to the world (Rom 8:33; 1 Pet 1:2; 2 Cor 5:17–20; Acts 1:8)

- The second coming of Jesus Christ and judgment of the world (Matt 24:3–25:46; 1 Thess 4:13–18; Rev 1:7, 20:11–15; Dan 12:2)

Creeds and statements of faith are many things, but one thing is certain: they are organizing systems. They represent an attempt to harmonize certain parts of Scripture and then claim that these representative parts reflect the message of the Bible.

Identifying, organizing, and systemizing texts in the Bible is engaging in biblical interpretation or "hermeneutics." Hermeneutics is often described as both the science and art of interpreting the Bible. It is a science because there are some challenges and difficulties as we approach the critical study of the New Testament, like the time gap from the documents written a long time ago to today, the historical and cultural gap between ours and the Eastern Mediterranean and Greco-Roman cultures, and the language or linguistic barrier between English and Hebrew and Koine Greek.

The first goal for the one attempting to interpret the Bible is to understand the story in its ancient context (as much as one possibly can) before attempting to apply its truths and ideas to our time, which is a second and important goal. Hermeneutics is believed to have artistic and creative elements in how the biblical text is translated and how meaning is drawn from it and applied to diverse audiences. There are many traditions in the church that emerge because of the influence of culture and individuality. Interpreters begin with the linguistic, literary, historical, and cultural aspects of the Bible and then make culturally and personally responsible conclusions about the meaning of the text and how it applies today. Hermeneutics as both the science and art of interpretation would suggest that the aim is to come away from the text with both a proper historical and theological understanding of its contents. But often hermeneutics can get one bogged down in the details of a single passage or biblical book. However, ultimately, employing solid hermeneutical principles should result in an understanding of the Bible's overall theological message as a group of writings.

The important point is that there is a working theological framework that Christians draw on, from teachings and stories that they use to interpret the life of faith. The debated issue is how this message is discerned or recognized, because many conservative interpreters continue to believe that their cultural lens is the only legitimate one. Christians will disagree and debate their understanding of the theological core, but there is no mistaking the fact that the core (however they define it) guides their approach to the selection of texts and the overall interpretation of Scripture. However, one would be mistaken to assume this is all there is to the interpretation of the Bible.

The Bible is Not an Ordinary Book

There is another reason the Bible is a different kind of book to interpret. Mystics, teachers, and scholars in different ages have long believed that there are spiritual dimensions to understanding the Bible. Let me explain. The Bible is both a simple and complex text. It can yield meaning to a child and yet also contains ideas that baffle scholars. It can be read devotionally, inspiring readers with stories of faith, courage, and endurance. The Bible can be read for instructional purposes, teaching about matters of faith, prayer, worship, and forgiveness. It can be studied historically as a text that chronicles the presence of ancient empires and cultures, particularly the history of Israel. However, the Bible is a religious text, a sacred text. Sacred texts are not just read and studied like other texts. They are revered because God is both the subject and influence in the writing (and collection) of the text. As such, the stories and teachings compiled in the Bible have a spiritual dimension that one must recognize and account for. Engaging the Bible is a different interpretative task than engaging other texts because one encounters the God whose inspirational activities form the backdrop of the text. The same God who inspired others to write also inspires readers. This is a dynamic not encountered in other texts.

Scripture has long been regarded as a pneumatic text in which one encounters the living voice of God. The word pneumatic comes from the Greek word *pneuma* which means "a current of air or a breeze." It is often translated as "spirit" in the New Testament (John 4:24; 2 Cor 7:1; Col 2:5). Interestingly, it can also be translated as "the wind" and conveys the idea of movement or a force that animates or moves material objects. Therefore, when I say that this multivolume book has pneumatic features, I mean the Holy Spirit works with, in, among, and around the biblical text to enable the reader to understand its contents and see its full import. African Americans from slavery to contemporary Pentecostal and Neo-Charismatic ministers speak of receiving revelations and insight into the meaning of the Bible. The belief in the Bible's pneumatic voice is not exclusively Pentecostal and Neo-Charismatic. But rather, Christian history provides abundant examples of the ways in which God's breath and presence are encountered in the words of the text and beyond as a result of reading or hearing the words of the text.

Augustine and later non-African church leaders, such as Martin Luther and John Wesley, all had "pneumatic-like" experiences or life changing "revelations" connected to reading Romans. Pneumatic experiences lead one to the biblical text to discover meaning or revelatory insight. In his treatise *The Confessions*, Augustine recalled weeping in the garden of his friend Alypius because of the wickedness of his life and hearing a child say, *"Tolle lege, tolle lege,"* which means "take up and read." He opened up a scroll and read this passage: "Not in carousing and drunkenness, not in sexual promiscuity and sensuality, not in strife and jealousy. But put on the Lord Jesus Christ and make no provision for the flesh in regard to its lusts." Augustine read this passage and confessed, "No further would I read, nor did I need; for instantly, as the sentence ended, a light, as it were, or security infused into my heart, and all the gloom of doubt vanished away."[3] The "voice" of the child pointed him to Scripture, and after an encounter with a passage from Scripture, he had a pneumatic experience that changed his life. His experience with this text, in particular, and the belief that this text was speaking to his existential predicament, illustrates the pneumatic dimensions of the Bible.

Origen, a third-century theologian from Alexandria, also recognized the Bible's pneumatic voice. What is implied by Scripture's pneumatic voice is the belief that the text contains layers of meaning that only the Holy Spirit can reveal and also that there are

3. Augustine, *Confessions*, 173–74.

manifold theological applications and implications that the Spirit reveals in studying and teaching. According to Origen, Scripture has an inner meaning that cannot be discerned by reading and studying the sacred text. In his treatise, *On First Principles,* he discussed this interesting aspect of understanding a "spiritual" text.

Origen taught that it is important to recognize the aim of the Spirit with regard to those who either cannot or will not diligently give themselves to these matters. He is describing a disposition that the reader must bring to the interpretive task. He explained that divine wisdom "has arranged for there to be certain stumbling blocks or interruptions of the narrative meaning." These stumbling blocks have two functions, "to shield the hidden or deeper meaning in the text and to oppose the reader and resultantly motivate the earnest student of the text to seek the inner meaning."[4] Origen also viewed Scripture as having both historical and futuristic relevance. He claimed that the Holy Spirit keeps the spiritual meaning either in what is bound to happen (future experience or event) or in what has already taken place in biblical history. A critical part of his understanding was that Scripture's inner meaning provided deeper insight into important historical moments in the Bible and even insight into events yet to come. In this sense, a narrative or what he called a "single verbal account" could convey multiple layers of meaning. But this inner meaning required spiritual illumination. Origen is often singled out for his belief that Scripture could convey layers of meaning and the creative and sometimes problematic ways he interpreted the Bible. His belief in Scripture's inner meaning is another example of the pneumatic dimensions of the Bible and its interpretation.

In the African American context, Scripture's pneumatic dimensions are often experienced individually through illumination or revelation and also in communally through preaching and storytelling as we experience the God who sides with the oppressed and downtrodden. By turning to Black preaching, I aim to emphasize the oral dimensions of interpretation and how interpretive meaning is connected to the experiential in the African American

4. Origen, "On First Principles, 2:9," 187.

religious context. The Bible is a core part of the language of faith that characterizes Black preaching. In the African religious milieu, which is an oral culture, the pneumatic speaks. Both the text and oral interpreter form a symbiotic and pneumatic voice heard by the people in the preaching moment. The Bible, as a pneumatic text, speaks in the preaching moment, and the people listen for and hear God's voice in the words and stories in Scripture. This weekly ritual of oral interpretation demonstrates the pneumatic dimensions of the Bible and worship in the African American context, a context permeated by the Spirit's activity.

The Bible has dual dimensions. It is an ancient text written in human languages by people from different cultures than ours about events they experienced. It is also a compilation of writings about God and God's work in ancient Israel and its surrounding regions. It climaxes in the life of Jesus and his death that became the launching pad for a broader program of divine activity. New Testament writers contended that God used these writings as a key part of his redemptive work in the world and opened their minds to understanding through the work of the Holy Spirit.[5]

The Importance of Discernment in Interpretation

Being selective with texts and the important truth that the Bible is a living and spiritual text illustrates the importance of discernment in the interpretation of the Bible, a neglected aspect in hermeneutics. The Greek word for discernment can be found in a text like 1 Cor 12. The word as a noun is *diakrisis*, which refers to "the ability to discriminate or distinguish, to differentiate, discern," and as a verb it is *diakrino*, which means "to evaluate, judge, recognize,

5. This aspect of interpretation is subjective and open to abuses, which is why many scholars ignore this aspect of biblical interpretation. However, the subjective nature of the Spirit's work in interpretation should not discount its importance. The methods and principles of biblical criticism have subjective elements, too. Higher and lower criticism still rely on the judgment of the interpreter and sources they choose to draw on and utilize. It does not discount their value in the interpretive enterprise. The point is all methods of interpretation have subjective elements.

discern, or to make a distinction between people." Paul used these words in relation to spiritual gifts, the discerning of spirits. For first century Christians, discernment was critical because of the preponderance of false prophets and teachers. The first apostles worked hard to lay groundwork that false teachers tried to build on or demolish with their teachings and ideas, often cloaked in the language of the Gospel. The apostles taught Christians that people may have gifts and even appear as an angel but have a spirit that is not of God and should rightly be recognized as such. In fact, one apostle taught churches to test or discern the spirits in teachers.

> Dear friends, do not believe every spirit, but test the spirits to see whether they are from God, because many false prophets have gone out into the world. This is how you can recognize the Spirit of God: Every spirit that acknowledges that Jesus Christ has come in the flesh is from God, but every spirit that does not acknowledge Jesus is not from God. This is the spirit of the antichrist, which you have heard is coming and even now is already in the world (1 John 4:1–3).

The point John is making is that a person's spirit—their deeper intentions, motives, and interests, are significant factors to consider. Since looks (what is external, physical) can be deceiving, discernment is an important spiritual matter.

Because discerning spirits is listed in 1 Cor 12 as a spiritual gift, it is right to recognize it as a product of the work of the Holy Spirit. Discernment works in the mind and heart of the Christian, enabling them to distinguish good from evil spirits (think internal influences). While this is a gift primarily related to people, it also has implications for the interpretation of the Bible. Surely the same Spirit that enables people to recognize ungodly influences in people can enable a person to distinguish texts (and interpretations) that edify from texts (and interpretations) that oppress. More importantly, discernment also refers to a spiritual insight required to understand the message in and behind the text. The Holy Spirit will help one to discern the life-giving message in the text.

What I am suggesting is that there is an element of discernment required to see the good news and truth of the Gospel in the matrix of stories, thousands of commandments, hundreds of characters, psalms, proverbs, and exhortations one reads in Scripture.[6] Without using discernment as an interpretive tool, one can understand the history, culture, languages, and people in the Bible but miss the deeper meaning that makes this text the word of God. Paul seemed to suggest this possibility in his first letter to the Corinthians. He argued in 1 Cor 1 that human wisdom does not always lead to an understanding of the truth of God. In fact, those who relied on human wisdom did not understand the cross and how it demonstrated the power of God to save. God chose something foolish to confound the wise and continues to do so. Paul tries to impress on his readers in Corinth the importance of the Spirit's work in giving discernment into spiritual things. It may help to see the pertinent verses in 1 Cor in both the traditional King James translation and a modern translation in order to maximize our understanding of what Paul is teaching.

6. I am making a theological statement here by placing the work of the Holy Spirit over the biblical text, a move that is critical to rescue Pentecostalism from the doctrines of inerrancy and infallibility that lift the biblical text to the place of God, an act that is idolatrous. This move is also a tacit rejection of humanism that claims the meaning of Scripture can be ascertained only through the tools of scientific inquiry. Without the Holy Spirit, both the fundamentalist and humanist are left in blindness, a point I will explain in the final chapter.

Now we have received, not the spirit of the world, but the spirit which is of God; that we might know the things that are freely given to us of God. Which things also we speak, not in the words which man's wisdom teacheth, but which the Holy Ghost teacheth; comparing spiritual things with spiritual. But the natural man receiveth not the things of the Spirit of God: for they are foolishness unto him: neither can he know them, because they are spiritually discerned (1 Cor 2:12–14 KJV).	What we have received is not the spirit of the world, but the Spirit who is from God, so that we may understand what God has freely given us. This is what we speak, not in words taught us by human wisdom but in words taught by the Spirit, explaining spiritual realities with Spirit-taught words. The person without the Spirit does not accept the things that come from the Spirit of God but considers them foolishness, and cannot understand them because they are discerned only through the Spirit (1 Cor 2:12–14 NIV).

Paul's juxtaposition between the natural and spiritual person was a way to identify this difference in the person operating with discernment. The natural person relies on human wisdom. There is great value in this, but it does not lead to the realization of the truth. The spiritual person, not discounting the value of human wisdom (because Paul was a highly educated person) but instead relying on the Spirit to give discernment, understands the message of God and the gospel of Jesus the Christ.

Discernment involves three actors: the Holy Spirit, the individual person, and the community of interpreters that influence their thinking. All three actors were involved at the church of Corinth. Discernment is not merely an individual insight but a product of an individual being intentionally formed by two other actors: the Holy Spirit and fellow believers. Yes, discernment is cultivated spiritually and communally through thoughtful study with fellow Christians. Let me explain how I learned to use discernment in interpretation.

I was baptized in the Spirit the summer of 1992 and have experienced since then an awareness of the inner voice or the unction of the Holy Spirit. For many this may sound strange, but for many like myslef, it is not. We believe it is a product of a spiritual relationship with God. It began for me with the discipline of reading and meditating on Scripture. I would read a passage, sometimes reading over the same passage multiple times. I would then enter into a time of reflection, praise, and prayer. Much of what was prayer was joy as my spirit was learning more about God, about others who walked the journey of faith, and about the path before me. It was humbling to know that God would include me in his great work and plan for all creation. Through the discipline of reading and memorizing large parts of Scripture, like my ancestors, the language of Scripture became a thought world and filter for my understanding of many things. What I experienced is actually taught in the Bible.

The Old Testament emphasizes the importance of internalizing the Scriptures in places like Deut 28:1; Josh 1:8; and Ps 119. Both Jesus and Paul talked about this as well. Jesus referred to the Scriptures as bread during his temptation with the devil and responded by repeating the importance of living by the word of God. The bread motif was an obvious reference to food, which is eaten and provides sustenance. Paul referenced this idea in Rom 12. He connected transformation with the renewal of the mind, which was another way to insist on the importance of internalizing Scripture. Scripture has to get so deep in you that it alters the way you think and live. It also proves to be the gateway for a deeper understanding of the Word. I learned to discern the voice of the Spirit. I am not claiming that God speaks directly to me like I speak to other humans. God does not. But there are times I sense God's presence and leading to quiet my mind and focus. What I sense in my spirit finds its way onto paper and into a season of prayer and meditation. In my youth there were times I was quick to share it and put these ideas into sermons. But over the years, I have learned that mature and responsible spirituality requires discipline and seasoning. So, I learned how to listen, and, unlike young Samuel who quickly (and mistakenly) ran to the high priest Eli, saying, "here I am for you called me," I sit with it, sometimes for years before ever preaching or teaching.

God also used "Spirit-filled" Christian scholars in a very direct way to open my eyes both to the meaning of the content in

Scripture and its implications for the church and world. I grew up in church. I attended a Pentecostal-Holiness church in Kimball, West Virginia during my early years. I learned about God, Jesus Christ, faith, testifying, singing, and shouting for hours on Sundays because God was good. I also entered Christian ministry in the Church of God in Christ where I was taught the importance of trusting in God regardless of circumstance, holiness, and respecting people God called to instruct me. I have taken these lessons with me. But two influences stand out in my mind. First, I also attended Faith Center, an African American nondenominational church that taught the importance of basing everything on the Word. It was the first Black church I attended that valued teaching on Sunday mornings. This church impacted me in significant ways because I had always believed that Christians should be more "Word" oriented. Faith Center valued communal teaching rather than the individual study of Scripture. My experience at Faith Center was good preparation for meeting Drs. Susan Garrett, Marion Soards, Stephen Ray, Dale Andrews, and Kathryn Johnson while a student at Louisville Seminary and later meeting Estrelda Alexander and Archie Wright while a student at Regent University. Collectively, they challenged me in foundational and advanced courses in New Testament, theology, and ministry to engage critically the whole text of Scripture and its interpretation as an act of faith and as an important part of the minister's calling to teach and preach the Word. They taught me "the who and what of the Bible and theology," but more importantly, they taught me "the why," as in why it matters and for whom it matters most—historically marginalized and excluded groups. God placed them in my life to help me as I grew in my understanding of my call to teach as a minister and scholar. Without them, I would not be where I am, for in different ways, they modeled principles that I write about in this book. Over the years I have now come to understand that discernment is not merely the result of praying before one reads and studies Scripture. Discernment is the product of a life filled with the Spirit of God, a mind that is both open to God and yielded to God, teachers, and systems of interpretation that take the whole of Scripture seriously. That is why studying Scripture with trained Christian scholars of the Bible, theologians, historians, ethicists, and ministry practitioners is so important for anyone wanting to do ministry. Discernment cannot be underestimated in the interpretation of Scripture, which, as I've argued, is no ordinary book. But the Bible is a book with difficult sections. It's to some of those "problematic texts" that we now turn.

Chapter Three

Problematic Texts in the Bible

MANY CHRISTIANS BELIEVE THAT the Bible is the word of God. I grew up hearing my uncles and aunts call it the "Good Book," which for them meant the Bible is the book that teaches you how to live a good life. This is true. The Bible teaches about a powerful and holy God who created the heavens and the earth. It teaches about the different ways people are called into relationship with God. The Bible talks about covenants, promises, obedience and blessings, disobedience and cursings, idolatry, abominations, sins and sin, redemption, atonement, adoption, justification, and salvation. It teaches ethics and morals such as neighbor love, showing kindness to strangers, giving to the poor, peacemaking, non-retaliation, forgiveness, patience, and self-control. It emphasizes the importance of justice in communities and gives readers a compelling vision of a new heaven and earth free from strife and suffering.

There is also a deeper belief here and a connection that makes reading the Bible a serious matter. When people call the Bible the Good Book, they believe that by reading and applying the teachings of the Bible, a believer can lead a life that is pleasing to God, not just a good life. The connection between the Bible and the divine will is significant. One reason this connection is made is because of a popular text in the Bible.

> All Scripture is inspired by God and profitable for
> teaching, for reproof, for correction, for training in

34

righteousness; so that the man of God may be adequate, equipped for every good work. (2 Tim 3:16–17 NASB)

I have heard this text used more times than I can count in the conservative churches of my formative years, and sadly, it has been misused and abused because of a misunderstanding of the word "all" at the beginning of this verse. Many read this verse and assume that everything in the Bible is useful without understanding two things. First, Paul was not referring to the writings of the New Testament when he said "all Scripture," but the Septuagint, the Bible of the first Christians. There was no New Testament when Paul wrote these words. He also did not see himself writing Scripture, but rather a letter to a young pastor. The Bible as we know with an Old and New Testament was not what Paul had in mind here, and so it is inaccurate to push this Scripture's applicability too far. Second and more importantly, the word "all" is a reference to Scripture in the aggregate, what it stands for and how it functions in the church. "All" is not a reference to all of the contents of the Bible being equally applicable.

A Helpful Distinction

This point cannot be overstated. Too many Christians read this verse in 2 Timothy and reach a faulty conclusion. They confuse the authoritative function of the Bible in the life of the church with the entirety of the contents of the Bible. The text as a whole holds a certain authority over the church and individual lives of Christians. However, it does not mean that every word or verse is equally applicable. Without understanding these two important points, one is left with false assumptions and inferences drawn from this popular verse that can complicate a person's understanding of some of what they read in the Bible. These assumptions can morph into beliefs that pervade the culture of conservative American Christianity. There is one colloquial expression very prominent in Evangelical and Pentecostal churches that equates every single word in the Bible, the preacher's interpretations, and sermons on verses in the Bible with God-speak. It is a claim to divine authority in the act of reading and preaching that is both dangerous and idolatrous. The expression, "God said it—I believe it—That settles it," is well-intended but again is based on the flawed assumption that everything in Scripture is generally good and equally applicable. Such an assumption is both incorrect and naïve. It is also a belief that non-Christians and persons of other faiths who read the Bible find to be problematic. While I wholeheartedly agree with the idea that the Bible is the Good Book, I also understand that this belief is based on a particular assumption about the entirety of the contents of the Bible—the Bible teaches how to love God, love one's neighbor, and live according to the divine will, etc. This may be the general tenor of Scripture but is not a reflection of all of its contents.

Simon Loveday's careful work on the Bible, interestingly titled *The Bible For Grown-Ups*, touches on the issue of some of the problematic parts of the Bible. In his discussion of the issue of the Old Testament and morality, he begins with very insightful questions: "What kind of god is God and what morality does the Old Testament teach? And is it right?" He begins by showing that a close look at the Old Testament reveals "that morally it is a very mixed bag."[1] He illustrates the "mixed moral bag" by listing ten statements. Nine are from the Old Testament; one is not.

1. "Therefore thus saith the Lord God . . . because of all thine abominations . . . the fathers shall eat the sons in the midst of thee, and the sons shall eat their fathers";

2. "Because thou servedest not the Lord thy God with joyfulness; and with gladness of heart . . . he shall put a yoke of iron upon thy neck, until he hath destroyed thee . . . The tender and delicate woman among you . . . her eye shall be evil toward the husband of her bosom, and toward her son, and toward her daughter, And toward her young one that cometh out from between her feet, and toward the children which she

1. Loveday, *Bible for Grown-Ups*, 29.

shall bear: for she shall eat them for want of all things secretly in the seige";

3. "Moreover the children of then strangers that do sojourn among you, of them shall ye buy, and of their families that are with you, which they beget in your land: and they shall be your possession. And ye shall take them as an inheritance for your children after you, to inherit them for a possession; they shall be your bondmen (slaves) for ever";

4. "If a man have a rebellious and stubborn son, which will not obey the voice of his father, or the voice of his mother . . . Then shall his father and his mother lay hold on him, and bring him out to the elders of his city, and to the gate of his place . . . And all the men of his city shall stone him with stones, that he die";

5. "For that which befalleth the sons of men befalleth beasts . . . as the one dieth the other; yea, they have all one breath; so that a man hath no pre-eminence above a beast: for all is vanity";

6. "Happy shall he be, that rewardeth thee as thou hast served us. Happy shall he be, that dasheth thy little ones against the stones";

7. "A gift in secret pacifieth anger: and a reward in the bosom, strong wrath";

8. "And he took it, and the king thereof, and all the cities thereof; and they smote them with the edge of the sword, and utterly destroyed all the souls that were therein; he left none remaining . . . but utterly destroyed all that breathed, as the Lord God of Israel commanded";

9. "And the fear of you and the dread of you shall be upon every beast of the earth, and upon every fowl of the air, upon all that moveth upon earth, and all the fishes of the sea; into your hand are they delivered";

10. "In the name of God, the lord of mercy, the giver of mercy. When God's help comes and He opens up your way, when

you see people embracing God's faith in crowds, celebrate the praise of your Lord and ask His forgiveness: He is always ready to accept repentance."[2]

Interestingly the statement about God's mercy is not found in the Old Testament. It turns out that statements one through nine are in the Bible while number ten is from the Qur'an. So, it would appear that what makes the Old Testament's moral vision mixed are texts like these.

The point is the Bible says other things besides "love thy neighbor" and "pray for one another that ye may be healed." It says things that will surprise and sometimes shock us. Scripture contains stories that are problematic, and these statements and stories are an important part of understanding why some people avoid sections of the Bible or do not read it at all. I referred to these texts as a reflection of the "dark side of the Bible" in my Introduction to the Biblical Literature course that I taught at Claflin University (HBCU). Michael Kerrigan uses the language of "dark history" in his study of many of the problematic texts in the Bible.[3] The language "dark side" of the Bible is not meant to be alarming but rather serves to highlight those texts in the Bible that are instructing or illustrating principles and ethics we would not commonly associate with the Bible—incest, holding slaves, beating slaves, killing people for sins, not marrying persons of other ethnicities, referring to non-Jewish persons as dogs or unclean persons, stoning families to death, etc.

Approaching Problematic Texts

Biblical texts become problematic because of what is said or taught about them. These texts are also complex, and it is not always easy to know whether these texts are applicable today, and if so, in what way. A helpful approach is first to identify these texts in the Bible.

2. Loveday, *Bible for Grown-Ups*, 30–31.
3. Kerrigan, *Dark History of the Bible*.

I categorize problematic texts in the Bible in seven ways as illustrated below.

Chart 4: Problematic Texts

Category	Sample Biblical Text(s)	Sample Verses (NIV)
(1) Texts issuing commands to participate in violence	1 Sam 15:1–3; Ps 137:9; Deut 20:1–20; Eccl 3:1, 3	This is what the Lord Almighty says: "I will punish the Amalekites for what they did to Israel when they waylaid them as they came up from Egypt. Now go, attack the Amalekites and totally destroy all that belongs to them. Do not spare them; put to death men and women, children and infants, cattle and sheep, camels and donkeys." (1 Sam 15:2–3)
(2) Texts that record stories of violence	Gen 4:1–12; Josh 8:18–31	Now Cain said to his brother Abel, "Let's go out to the field." While they were in the field, Cain attacked his brother Abel and killed him. (Gen 4:8)
(3) Texts that specifically regulate and support slavery	Eph 6:5–9; 1 Cor 7:21–23; 1 Tim 6:1–2	Slaves, obey your earthly masters with respect and fear, and with sincerity of heart, just as you would obey Christ. Obey them not only to win their favor when their eye is on you, but as slaves of Christ, doing the will of God from your heart. (Eph 6:5–6)

(4) Texts that record stories with slaves and/or use slave language and ideology	Matt 8:5–10; Luke 12:35–48	"The servant who knows the master's will and does not get ready or does not do what the master wants will be beaten with many blows . . . " (Luke 12:47)
(5) Texts issuing commands to silence or marginalize women	1 Cor 14:34–35; 1 Tim 2:11–15	Women should remain silent in the churches. They are not allowed to speak, but must be in submission, as the law says. If they want to inquire about something, they should ask their own husbands at home; for it is disgraceful for a woman to speak in the church. (1 Cor 14:34–35)
(6) Texts that record stories of the oppression and or marginalization of women	Judg 11:29–40 and 19:1–30; 2 Sam 13:1–19; Matt 15:21–28	Leaving that place, Jesus withdrew to the region of Tyre and Sidon. A Canaanite woman from that vicinity came to him, crying out, "Lord, Son of David, have mercy on me! My daughter is demon-possessed and suffering terribly." . . . The woman came and knelt before him. "Lord, help me!" she said. He replied, "It is not right to take the children's bread and toss it to the dogs. "Yes it is, Lord," she said. "Even the dogs eat the crumbs that fall from their master's table." (Matt 15:21–27)

(7) Texts that specifically condemn or prohibit practices debated by Christian Churches such as divorce, war, tithing, homosexuality, suicide, and eternal damnation or hell.	Luke 16:18; Exod 20:13; Mal 3:8–11; Rom 1:24–28; Dan 12:2, Matt 25; and Rev 20:11–15; 21:8	"Anyone who divorces his wife and marries another woman commits adultery, and the man who marries a divorced woman commits adultery . . . " (Luke 16:18)

These seven categories provide a way to identify statements and organize them as problematic according to their content rather than labeling them problematic for being recorded in the first place. It does not necessarily mean these verses are all rejected outright; though, many are rightly rejected as reflections of divine will. Identifying them as problematic let's us know they require great care when interpreting for one's life and others in the world. The categories are not intended to solve problems but rather introduce a way to begin to identify certain texts as problematic and less helpful or worthy of use in preaching and teaching to others. After all, just because the Bible says something, does not always mean we should do it. Some statements require thought and explanation and not necessarily action.

Scholars use several methods to identify these texts. For example, Phyllis Trible uses the language of "texts of terror" to describe four stories in the Bible where women suffer in profound ways—the stories of Hagar, Tamar, the unnamed woman, and Jephthah's daughter in the Old Testament. Her description of these passages in the Bible is both alarming and instructive about the ways certain texts have been a part of the history of abuse women have endured at the bloody hands of the church.

> Indeed, they are tales of terror with women as victims. Belonging to the sacred scriptures of synagogue and church, these narratives yield four portraits of suffering in ancient Israel: Hagar, the slave used, abused, and rejected; Tamar, the princess raped and discarded; an

unnamed woman, the concubine raped, murdered, and dismembered; and the daughter of Jephthah, a virgin slain and sacrificed.[4]

She writes to instruct readers to approach such texts with care so as not to utilize texts to terrorize and further marginalize women today. Trible's aim here informs the approach I take with the issue of problematic texts. The point is not to replicate practices that are harmful to persons and communities, which requires wrestling with some texts, learning different ways to use them, or in some cases not to use them at all. None of this is possible unless the reader is cognizant of the fact that the good book says a few problematic things.

Even journalists are weighing in on the issue of problematic texts in the Bible and the moral and theological problems one has when thinking about statements made or things directed by God. In Joe Kovacs's book *Shocked by The Bible*, Kovac discusses a very interesting topic, "The Biggest Killer in the Bible" (ch. 15), framing the issue as follows:

> From start to finish, corpses seem to pile up everywhere in Scripture. Readers find numerous accounts of murder, execution, human sacrifice, war-related casualties, natural disasters such as famines and earthquakes, and the ever-popular "dropping dead." But who is the biggest killer in the Bible? The fact is that it's God Himself. Scripture states that God ordered capital punishment for men, women, and even young children—sometimes in very large numbers. It may disturb modern people (especially opponents of capital punishment), but thousands, perhaps millions, of human beings experienced death either by God's direct hand or His edict.[5]

In a subsection he titles "The Death Toll," Kovac gives detailed accounts of stories of God-initiated violence in the Bible. The sheer volume and details are staggering to read and process.

4. Trible, *Texts of Terror*, 1.
5. Kovacs, *Shocked By The Bible*, 123.

I have organized his findings in what follows as a useful guide for further study.

The Biggest Killer in the Bible

The largest mass execution in world history occurred in the great Flood of Noah's time, recorded in Genesis. The entire global population—with the exception of Noah, his wife, and their three sons and their wives—drowned when God flooded the world with water. [Quotes Gen 7:23]. God spared only Noah's immediate family. Every other person, numbering perhaps into the millions, was killed by God. Even unborn children in the womb never got to see the light of day due to the deluge. The reason: "God saw that the wickedness of man was great in the earth, and that every imagination of the thoughts of his heart was only evil continually. And it repented the Lord that he had made man on the earth, and it grieved him at his heart" (Gen 6:5–6).

Later two residents of two ancient cities, found guilty of "very grievous" sin, suffered scorching deaths at the direct hand of God. "The Lord rained upon Sodom and upon Gomorrah brimstone and fire from the Lord out of heaven" (Gen 19:24). God also turned executioner during the time of the Exodus from Egypt—the Bible records that a massive plague snuffed out the lives of all the firstborn children of Egypt, while God spared the Israelites. [Quotes Exod 11:4–7].

But God's wrath was not limited to pagans living in Egypt. Once his own people were freed from captivity, they quickly engaged in sinful behavior, creating an idol in the form of a golden calf. When Moses descended Mount Sinai and discovered the rebellious activity, he was ordered by God to execute those who chose not to be on the Lord's side—an estimated three thousand men. [Quotes Exod 32:27–28].

During the Israelites' time in the wilderness and their takeover of the promised land, they received divine orders to kill men, women, children, and animals. [Quotes Num 21:33–35].

When Israelite men began having sex with Moabite women and adopted heathen practices such as bowing down and sacrificing to false gods, God became angry enough to slay some twenty-four thousand of his own people, most of whom were executed by hanging: "And the Lord said unto Moses, Take all the heads of the people, and hang them up before the Lord against the sun, that the fierce anger of the Lord may be turned away from Israel . . . And those that died in the plague were twenty and four thousand" (Num 25:4, 9).

THE BIBLE IN THE ASHES OF SOCIAL CHAOS

When God exacted revenge against the Midianites who fought against his people, Moses was surprised to see women and children alive. So, he ordered the slaughter of all nonvirgin women and male children [quotes Num 31:17].

God ordered the destruction of Sihon and his descendants who fought against the Israelites. Note that even the little children were not spared: [quotes Deut 2:34].

God later explained that he did not want any pagan left alive to corrupt Israel. He would obviously not get the gold star from today's "tolerance" crowd. [Quotes Deut 20:16–18].

When the walls of ancient Jericho came crashing down at the blast of trumpets, Joshua and his men spared no one: [quotes Josh 6:21].

Some twelve thousand were slain as God made Joshua's army victorious at a place called Ai: [quotes Josh 8:24–25].

As Joshua's fighting men were killing enemies in battle, God himself got involved, firing weapons from the sky and killing more people than Joshua's army: [quotes Josh 10:11]. The point is made over and over again. God does get angry, and he kills men, women, and children, some of whom never even heard of him. And His anger is not just an Old Testament phenomenon.[6]

Kovacs's work lays out in detail a host of very disturbing texts in the Bible where God is a primary perpetrator of violence. If the language and exhortation of 2 Timothy is brought to bear on texts like these, it could result in interpretations and teachings that would be problematic to say the least.

"Problematic" Interpretation of Problematic Texts

Trible's approach of flagging "texts of terror" or problematic texts so readers do not replicate particular actions and instructions in the Bible is not always followed by scholars and pastors. Some are compelled to use them. Whether you believe it or not, some of these problematic texts have been and continue to be interpreted in ways that support illegal and unethical practices like murder and slavery. The justification for it is always framed in a religious

6. Kovacs, *Shocked By the Bible*, 123–27.

manner, but in the end, practices like human enslavement and actions like killing are endorsed by very prominent pastors and theologians past and present. I will give two examples.

One prominent Baptist minister, Thorton Stringfellow, argued that the references to servants (slaves) in the Bible meant that God approved of the practice of African enslavement in the 1800s and slavery for all time. His interpretation was built on a string of problematic texts about slaves.

> God decreed this relation between the posterity of Canaan and the posterity of Shem and Japheth from passages including Genesis 9:25-27 . . . God executed this decree by aiding the posterity of Shem (at a time when "they were holiness to the Lord"), to enslave the posterity of Canaan in the days of Joshua (Genesis 7:5; 12:15-16; 14:14; 23:6) . . . God ratified the covenant of promise with Abraham, he recognized Abraham as the owner of slaves he had bought with his money and recorded his approbation of the relation, by commanding Abraham to circumcise them (Genesis 17:12-13) . . . When he took Abraham's posterity by the hand in Egypt, five hundred years afterward, he publicly approbated the same relation, by permitting every slave they had bought with their money to eat the Passover, while he refused the same privilege to their hired servants (Exodus 12:44-45) . . . God, as their national lawgiver, ordained by express statute, that they should buy slaves of the nations around them (the seven devoted nations excepted), and that these slaves and their increase should be a perpetual inheritance to their children (including Leviticus 25:44-46) . . . God ordained slavery by law for their captives taken in war, while he guaranteed a successful issue to their wars, so long as they obeyed him (Deuteronomy 20:10-11) . . . when Jesus ordered his gospel to be published through the world, the relation of master and slave existed by law in every province and family of the Roman Empire, as it had done in the Jewish commonwealth for fifteen hundred years (citing Gibbon, with Matthew 28:19; 1 Corinthians 7:21) . . . Jesus ordained, that the legislative authority, which created this relation in that

45

empire, should be obeyed and honored as an ordinance
of God, as all government is declared to be (Romans
13:7; 1 Peter 2:17–18) . . . Jesus has prescribed the mutual
duties of this relation in his kingdom (1 Timothy 6:2–5)
. . . in the Apostolic churches, Jesus orders that fellowship
shall be disclaimed with all such disciples, as seditious
persons- whose conduct was not only dangerous to the
State, but destructive to the true character of the gospel
dispensation.[7]

He concluded by adamantly stating that the one "who believes the
Bible to be of divine authority, believes those laws were given by
the Holy Ghost to Moses" (and other biblical authors) must accept
that God "has given them his sanction, therefore, they must be
in harmony with his moral character."[8] This is but one of many
examples of this kind of interpretation in Christian history. Christians for centuries have used the Bible to justify the practice of
human enslavement and even argued that God ordained certain
persons to perpetual enslavement.

In a classic text written by R. A. Torrey, former dean of
Moody Bible Institute and a prominent evangelist of the early
1900s, he takes on the text of 1 Sam 15. At first, he admits the
difficult nature of such a text and even alludes to Deuteronomy
20:16–17, which calls for the complete destruction of the Hittites,
Amorites, Canaanites, Perizittes, Hivites, and Jebusites. He then
moves to explain why God would do this.

Let us say, first of all, that it is certainly appalling that
any people would be utterly put to the sword, not only
the men of war, but also the old men and old women, as
well as the young women and children. Yet there is something more appalling than even this, when one stops to
think about the matter, and that is that the iniquity of any
people would have become so full, their rebellion against
God so strong and so universal, their moral corruption
and debasement so utter and so pervasive, even down to
babies just born, as to make such treatment absolutely

7. Stringfellow, "Bible Argument or Slavery," 461–92.
8. Stringfellow, "Bible Argument or Slavery," 461–92.

necessary in the interests of humanity . . . We learn, not
only from the Bible but also from other sources, how un-
fathomable were the depths of moral pollution to which
these nations had sunk. They had become a moral cancer, threatening the very life of the whole human race.
That cancer had to be cut out in every fiber if the body
was to be saved . . . Similarly the kindest thing that God
could do for the human race was to cut out this cancer in
every root and every fiber.[9]

Here in the clearest way possible, a prominent Christian thinker
and pastor, endorses this violence as acceptable—"The people
were so evil that God had to direct Samuel in this manner." He
even frames their slaughter as an act of kindness on the behalf of
God. Is this the message of the Bible? Does this reflect the God of
the Bible? Stringfellow and Torrey answer "yes," but I say "no."

I will say three things about this. First, Stringfellow's theology,
where every verse is equally applicable and reflective of the divine
will left him no choice but to flatten and systematize verses en-
dorsing slavery in the Bible. Second, Torrey's thinking is shared by
many Christians today. In my "Introduction to Biblical Literature"
class, the deeper the grounding the students had in the church, the
more likely they were to justify and accept violence as the divine
will. I recall being utterly amazed by student papers on this topic. I
was both amazed and disappointed by their ability to justify murder in the name of God and how instrumental the church has been
in forming their thinking in this regard. Third and more importantly, this kind of interpretation is dangerous given the influence
of the Bible in the world. When a text like this is endorsed and not
corrected, it is the equivalent of giving sanction to these actions.
Sadly, there is a long history of interpreters going to great lengths
to do this—slavery is God's will, or some people have to be killed as
an act of kindness by God. These absurd conclusions are again the
result of a hermeneutic where every verse is equal and applicable
in the same way. I hope my readers will remember this before they
react with the old belief that asserts every verse is the word of God

9. Torrey, *Difficulties in the Bible*, 68–69.

and profitable for instruction in righteousness. All texts are not useful—some merely provide filler information that is rarely given any attention while others make statements giving divine sanction to violence, misogyny, and slavery. The implicit and explicit claims of such texts are not binding in a way texts that speak of God's love and justice are, because these verses point to much broader truths. Many verses in the Bible are useful but not in the same way, which is why great care must be taken in interpretation, especially when it involves problematic texts.

Problematic Texts and History

There are two aspects to this issue of problematic texts in the Bible: (1) problematic statements and stories in the biblical text; and (2) the problematic ways such statements and stories are interpreted. The first aspect has gained importance because more people are made aware of these texts in this age of social media and information technology. Knowing the existence of extremely problematic texts in the Bible discourages thoughtful and religious people from reading it. For some, the very presence of these texts is the reason they do not believe the Bible is good and inspired by God. These texts also embolden atheism and unbelief as more non-Christians raise questions about the beliefs of Christians and the writings they hold dear because these texts raise difficult religious, ethical, and interpretive questions that are not easily answered. For example, "Do problematic texts mean that the Bible cannot be the word of God because it contains these references and teachings?" "Should Christians just ignore those passages and stories in the Bible?" And the most important question is, "Does it mean the Bible and the Christian God sanction violence, slavery, and ethnic prejudice, etc.?" There is great value in giving space for questions like this and giving answers that are honest, measured, critical, yet reverent.

The second aspect of the darker side of the Bible is historical. There is a long and painful history of oppression, violence, and death connected to the Bible. The church taught love and forgiveness. Churches also took problematic texts and did deplorable

48

things in the name of God. How these texts have been interpreted by Christians and churches for centuries is a point that cannot be dismissed and treated in an ancillary manner. And yet, that is exactly what happens. This aspect of interpreting Bible is often ignored. The truth is there are texts in the Bible that have been interpreted and acted upon in ways that resulted in people's deaths, enslavement for centuries, exclusion from ministry, the destruction of the environment, even domestic and child abuse. John Spong, an Episcopal bishop, wrote a book discussing this and provides a helpful introduction to this issue.

> In the history of the Western world, however, this Bible has also left a trail of pain, horror, blood and death that is undeniable. Yet this fact is not often allowed to rise to consciousness. Biblical words have been used not only to kill, but even to justify that killing. This book has been relentlessly employed by those who say they believe it to be the God's Word, to oppress others who been, according to those believers, defined in the "hallowed" pages of this text as somehow subhuman. Quotations from the Bible have been cited to bless the bloodiest of wars. People committed to the Bible have not refrained from using the cruelest forms of torture on those whom they believe to have been revealed as the enemies of God in these "sacred scriptures".[10]

Spong's statement, "not often allowed to rise to consciousness" is particularly instructive because it highlights the church's role in suppressing this aspect of the Bible's history and influence. It is possible that Christians do not know these statements are in the Bible because of high rates of biblical illiteracy. Remember too many Christians over-utilize Sunday sermons as their sole means of reading the Bible. His suggestion that the church suppressed and minimized this painful history is accurate. I believe the reason some Christians suppress this history is because they do not want people to lose faith in the Bible's ability to speak on spiritual issues. I have found that more conservative churches ignore problematic

---

10. Spong, *Sins of Scripture*, 4.

texts fearing that they undermine the credibility of the Bible as the "God-breathed," inerrant, and authoritative word on matters of faith and life, while more liberal thinkers, particularly in university and college settings, use problematic texts to attack the "naïve" belief in the Bible as the literal word of God. My aim in this study is not to join the discourse that seeks to divinize or weaponize the Bible but rather explore ways to address problematic texts in the Bible in both a reverent and critical manner. Whatever the reasons are, churches and their ministers have done the Bible a great disservice by hiding or exploiting this aspect of its history from thoughtful readers of faith and unbelief.

The painful history Spong mentions is directly connected to these problematic texts in the Bible. Texts in the Bible have been read and utilized in a way to justify Holy War (the crusades, killing people who taught against the church), genocide (killing brown-skinned people often called pagans, heathens, and or atheists), anti-Semitism (persecution of Jewish persons and the Holocaust), European colonialism and American slavery, and centuries of oppression of women and dark-skinned persons. Even today, texts in Rom 1 and 13 are used to deny gay persons rights as United States citizens, to exclude them from churches, and to justify separating Mexican immigrant children from their parents.

There are stories and teachings in the Bible that some find difficult to hear—"kill the women and children," "women keep silent in church," or "slaves obey your masters." These texts and their histories in the church have had a devastating effect on nations, communities, large and small, for generations, which is why Spong sought to expose what he calls "terrible texts" or "texts of hate." Much work has been done on issues such as slavery, the oppression of women, violence in the Bible, and war because the Christian church has such a painful legacy around these issues. With the increasing numbers of non-Christians in society and the pervasive influence of social media outlets like YouTube, Christians today cannot avoid this history, nor the issue of problematic texts and the questions people have about this and the Bible itself.

Historic Responses to Problematic Texts in the Bible

I am not the first person to attempt this. As a matter of fact, I am part of a tradition experienced in dealing with problematic texts in our sacred book and life of faith. During the years leading up to the Civil War, African American Christians found the Bible to be a complex document and adopted creative ways to engage its promises and perils. I have studied this history for nearly a decade and found it to be instructive. In particular, Allan Callahan's study of African Americans and the Bible has proven to be one of the best studies of the difficulties faced by enslaved Africans as they negotiated their introduction to the Bible.[11] I am convinced they had a healthy understanding of the Bible, and I am equally convinced it is an understanding sorely needed in Pentecostal and Charismatic churches today.

African American Christians understand that there are good and bad messages in the Bible. Historically, the Bible was an important part of the life of faith for Black Christians, and so discarding Scripture entirely was often not an option. For example, Frederick Douglass retorted, "the Bible is not a bad book because those who profess to believe the Bible are bad." He goes on to ask, "Shall we therefore fling the Bible away as a pro-slavery book?"[12] The implication here is clear. Douglass claimed that they would not discard the Bible. However, their decision to hold on to the Bible was not just based on white abuses and misinterpretations. They held to the Bible because they recognized and embraced its complexities. Allen Callahan's book, *The Talking Book*, notes that for some enslaved Africans, the Bible was a "poison book," meaning there were things stated and verses in the Bible used to justify their enslavement and exploitation as chattel. Callahand comments, "Though African Americans early discerned a spirit of justice in the Bible, they discovered in the same moment that the letter of Holy Writ was sometimes at war with its spirit."[13] Blacks discovered that the

11. See Callahan, *Talking Book*.
12. Douglass, "Writings," 177.
13. Callahan, *Talking Book*, 25.

same book can tell a story of a God freeing slaves yet teach slaves to obey their masters. In a sense, African Americans realized that the Bible has ideological and theological contradictions. The poisonous applications of the Bible had a devastating effect on their lives as enslaved persons. Yet, many African Americans learned to hold to the Bible and wrestle with parts of its contents, because they accepted the fact that a sacred text has good and bad messages.

During the centuries of African enslavement, Black people learned to selectively appropriate portions of Scripture. *Selective appropriation* or interpretation was a tacit admission that not all statements and parts of scripture are useful for teaching and living. One of the more prominent examples of this practice by enslaved Africans comes from the grandmother of Howard Thurman. The following quote illustrates the selective appropriation of Scripture in light of oppressive texts in the Bible.

> I asked her one day why it was that she would not let me read any of the Pauline letters. What she told me I shall never forget. During the days of slavery she said the master's minister would occasionally hold services for the slaves. Old man McGhee was so mean that he would not let a Negro minister preach to his slaves. Always the white minister used as his text something from Paul. At least three or four times a year he used as a text, "slaves be obedient to them that are your masters . . . as unto Christ." Then he would go on to show how it was God's will that we were slaves and how, if we were good and happy slaves, God would bless us. I promised my Maker that if I ever learned to read and freedom came I would not read that part of the Bible. Since that fateful day on the front porch in Florida I have been working on the problem her words presented.[14]

In some instances, like the one described by Thurman, certain texts were simply ignored or not used by formerly enslaved Africans. They were selectively appropriating texts, which is actually a veiled rejection of some texts and their authoritative bearing on their understanding of God and human flourishing.

14. Thurman, *Jesus and the Disinherited*, 30–31.

Another common African American response to problematic biblical texts was *counter-interpretation*. Sometimes, rather than ignoring a passage or part of the Bible, African American readers would turn to another text to correct or give a different meaning to the difficult passage. The practice of counter-interpretation helped them retain the Bible as their authoritative text while also recognizing that some parts were not binding or useful. So, in the face of texts like Gen 9 and 1 Cor 7:21, African Americans would turn to Gen 1 and the Exodus story to find words of healing, empowerment, and justice. Their selection of passages was grounded in their distinct understanding of God and the world. Counter-interpretation teaches that both their understanding of God and cultural situations affects how they interpret the Bible—select texts, discard texts, invest certain texts with more authority than other texts, and use them as a basis to ground their faith and emerging theology.

This history teaches that African American Christians learned to wrestle and struggle with bad texts. They did not explain them away. Instead, when on the occasion a text in Scripture was ignored, the decision to to do so was based on the knowledge of the text's content and claims. African American Christians reecognized that bad messages could be used to do horrible things, including dehumanize and exploiting persons created in the image of God. It was a part of the painful reality of using the same Bible their oppressors used. Many enslaved readers held to the Bible as the word of God even though doing so required them to struggle with the text in extraordinary ways.

These struggles with the Bible's problematic texts highlight two tensions in the Black religious tradition that can help Pentecostals today. The first tension is the acceptance of Scripture as an authoritative and reliable witness of sacred teaching. If the text is important enough to hold the title "word of God" or "Scripture" it should be read thoroughly, memorized, and drawn on deeply in preaching and worship. It is not just a religious symbol. It is a living text that should engage the best energies of mind and spirit. The second tension is the rejection of texts and interpretations used to sanction oppression or violence. A guiding principle is that God is good and does not ordain suffering. As oppressed persons, enslaved readers of the Bible knew the pain of religiously sanctioned violence. They were intimately acquainted with interpretations of texts that misrepresented God and the Gospel. They learned not to replicate these forms of interpretation. African American Christians in our country's history learned to navigate competing poles and they offer examples of such practice for us today.

Wrestle with the Text

The African American Christian tradition gifted me with the resources to teach my students how to be brutally honest with the Bible and its interprertation and yet also hold to it as sacred text. Because of the many problematic texts and interpretation, it is true that some persons and traditions reject the Bible outright as an authoritative guide. Nevertheless, I encourage them to wrestle with these texts. The idea of wrestling reveals an intimacy of engagement worthy of something that is as important as the Bible. We cannot ignore nor explain away problematic passages in the Bible without wrestling with them. It is ok to admit the Bible contains problematic texts. This is the first and most important step in the process of learning how to interpret these texts in a way that respects the Bible as Scripture while also not trying to use texts advocating things that are unethical, unjust, and harmful to persons.

In the end, wrestling with problematic texts shows thoughtful persons, many who are not Christians, that faith and intellectual honesty can work together for those of us who hold Scripture as the word of God. One need defend troubling passages to remain faithful to Scripture. I teach my students; my former professors taught me; and a long line of forebears taught us and modeled for us the need for wrestling with the Bible. This way of engaging Scripture is sorely needed in Pentecostal and Charismatic churches that too often view the Bible in its entirety as a textbook or rulebook directly from God, ignoring the import and impact of problematic passages.

Chapter Four

Interpreting Problematic Texts

DISCARDING PROBLEMATIC TEXTS IS certainly an option. Some Christians discard them wholesale and move on. I challenge my students, instead, to wrestle with the text and its interpretations. In order to make hermeneutical sense of problematic texts, a model of some kind is needed that teaches the interpreter how to organize and understand the plethora of texts contained in the Bible. A good place to begin is with some general rules. It is important to remember these preliminary suggestions before turning to an in-depth examination of how readers might rectify and provide meaning to problematic and sometimes conflicting texts in the Bible. These general rules are put into play along with our understanding of God and our ideas of what is good and just.

Guard against the tendency to read into the text. Interpretation begins first with what the text says before proceeding to discern what is implied. Focusing on what is said in its historical and literary contexts is critical and far too often missed in one's haste to ascribe meaning to what one has read and studied. It is equally important to recognize what the text does not say. Often people wrongly claim the Bible states something when it does not. This is important because a part of what one believes the text implies is influenced by personal factors such as one's cultural location, personal bias, and pre-understandings. Some implications are easy to discern, and some are not. Readers should be careful not to force an implication and they should always be humble about implications drawn from a text. It is surprising how many mistakes can be prevented by carefully beginning with an understanding of what the text actually says.

Do not use and systematize every verse but do not easily dismiss verses that challenge us. Interpretation breaks down with attempts to flatten all texts. Every verse, teaching, or story is not equally applicable. Recognizing this is critical and does not in any way undermine the authority of Scripture. Flatly interpreting all texts will invariably box the interpreter in with contradictory claims and assertions, and sometimes this lead to unjust and immoral acts like killing persons and marginalizing groups of people, for example. It can also result in interpretations that contradict other texts. For instance, one can believe what Jesus teaches on divorce and be left with the contradiction of a God who forgives all sins except for specific ones deemed unforgiveable. Or, as another example, one can accept Exodus 20 that killing is wrong and yet also look to verses that command people to kill. This is why discernment is so important in interpretation.

But, avoid getting bogged down with attempts to use and or systematize every verse in the Bible. Some texts in the Bible are no longer binding and should not be employed in interpretations (read the book of Leviticus!). There are three related and often overlapping reasons for this: (1) For dispensational purposes: Some texts reflect beliefs and practices from a past time when God was understood in different ways. These texts can be instructive (examples of things not to do, how things used to be, etc.). (2) For cultural purposes: Some instructions are limited to ancient cultural mores and beliefs like polygamy, dress, and treating women like property. There may be relevant applications but carrying over certain cultural practices is neither helpful nor accurate to the overall intent and purposes of the Bible as a sacred religious text. (3) For moral purposes: Some actions recorded in the Bible and perpetrated by persons considered heroes and heroines of the faith are simply immoral and illegal today. They are not paradigmatic for Christians today to follow in a straightforward manner. It is equally important to realize that we may not like or agree with ideas and teachings in some texts but that does not mean the text is not spiritually and morally binding on us as canonical Scripture. That is, not all texts can be too easily discarded or categorized as no longer binding for Christians today.

Do not assume the way a church or denomination selects, omits, organizes, and gives meaning to texts is God's way or God's truth. Such an assumption is both arrogant and idolatrous. Our interpretations of the Bible should strive to be faithful to God, the gospel of Jesus Christ, and the traditions we are a part of. But they are not unfiltered reflections of God's thinking.

The Spirit versus Letter of the Text

> Woe to you, teachers of the law and Pharisees, you hypocrites! You give a tenth of your spices—mint, dill and cumin. But you neglected the more important matters of the law—Justice, mercy, faithfulness. You should have practiced the latter, without neglecting the former. You blind guides! You strain out a gnat but swallow a camel. (Matt 23:23–24 ESV)

> He has made us competent as ministers of a new covenant—not of the letter but of the Spirit; for the letter kills, but the Spirit gives life. (2 Cor 3:6 ESV)

Like the teachers of the law and Pharisees described in Matthew, I used to flatly interpret Scripture and insist that every verse was inspired and applicable for Christian living. There were times I taught things that were oppressive and inconsistent with the character of God. For example, there was a time I insisted people had to be immersed at baptism or they would go to hell. I preached the letter! Like these teachers and Pharisees, I strained at gnats and swallowed camels because I ignored the weightier matters in the Bible. This was one of the reasons I eventuall attended seminary. I needed to learn how to rightly divide the material in the Bible. I needed to make sense of my sacred texts in a way that was life-giving in interpretation, preaching, and teaching.

Over the past decade as a seminary and doctoral student, a small church pastor, and later a biblical scholar, I learned how to do this. I learned to do what Paul rightly called dividing the word of truth. For me, it has meant learning how to differentiate "the letter that kills" (sometimes literally) in the text from "the spirit that gives life in the words of the text." For Paul, the comparison between the letter and spirit was a way to distinguish the deeper intent of the law. Paul was making a distinctly hermeneutical move with the law and his evolving understanding of God's work in the person of Jesus and the new communities forming around his teachings. I believe Paul's use of "spirit" and "letter" is instructive for modern interpreters of the sacred text. It is our task to distinguish the letter (often leading to texts that kill) from the spirit (texts that give life).

In my work as a biblical scholar, I have learned to discern what I call the "core theological message in Scripture." Discerning or identifying this message is a critical part of the interpretation of the broader meaning of Scripture. Like the Pharisees in Matt 23, who were blind to the weightier matters of the law, a person can read the contents of the Bible and not discern the deeper "theological" message. Sadly, this is widespread, especially in conservative church circles with which I am familiar. I was first introduced to this more discerning approach by William Swartley's work on slavery. Swartley shows how the Bible can say "yes" and "no" to controversial issues. However, just because the Bible can be used to defend something like slavery does not mean the interpretation is good.

Knowing this, one of the points Swartley makes is that the basic moral and theological principles of the entire Bible should be given authority and priority. Specific statements can stand in tension with these overarching principles and/or with other conflicting specific texts on the subject.[1] Interpreters use the core message to guide decisions about individual texts containing problematic statements, not jumping through hermeneutical hoops defending claims that are not worthy of God and the good news of Jesus.

1. Swartley, *Slavery, Sabbath, War, and Women*, 61.

Moving toward an understanding of the deeper theological meaning in the Bible is a twofold process that always begins with the sincere attempt to be faithful to the truth of God and the good news of Jesus Christ. This means one must, in some way, take a reverent, respectful approach to the Bible as a religious text and its ability to contain truth about God and Jesus Christ. As a religious text, it should be approached, read, and used with great care.

The second and more practical step is to carefully discern the stories and instructions contained in the Bible that teach persons how to be faithful witnesses of the Holy One in the world. The interpreter needs to discern the core theological message of the Bible and use it to guide interpretation for teachings and preaching. One has to be able to distinguish the forest (the overall theological message of Scripture) from the trees (individual stories and texts). Again, this approach is not new. Read the creeds, confessions, and statements of faith by various Christian churches and traditions. They discern and draw on select texts and craft faith statements they believe reflect the core message of the Bible.

Interpreting Problematic Texts in the Bible

Estrelda Alexander, an African American Pentecostal theologian, provides a helpful model of how to critically engage the Bible, even in light of problematic texts. She utilizes Scripture, including problematic texts about women, in her work as a political theologian. Her method provides a critical, honest, and reverent assessment of the text. Contrary to what some non-Christian scholars teach in some university settings, people of faith can critically study the Bible and find ways to appropriate its theological messages without accepting beliefs and practices that many consider unjust.

In a lecture on political theology, Alexander spells out interpretive principles for a "socio-political" interpretation of Scripture that is applicable for hermeneutics.[2] For Alexander, a socio-political reading of a text has two objectives: one is deconstructive

2. Alexander, "Political Theology and Hermeneutics," 2–4.

in nature and the other is constructive in nature. First, it seeks to provide a critical and honest assessment of the text and how it has been interpreted. An important part of this task is to identify the way that the text and interpretation are liberating, redemptive, and prophetic. It is equally important to have an honest recognition of the ways in which the texts were used to support injustice, oppression, and capitualtion to the ethos of the day (i.e., supporting fallen structures), and hence how texts were non-liberating, non-redemptive, and non-prophetic.

Second, this kind of interpretation seeks to find constructive ways to develop theologies and practices from both the liberating and non-liberating components. Part of this task entails identifying the reality of human blindness and sinfulness, especially in communities of faith that are complicit in injustice to the interpretive process. Such recognition serves to safeguard against pride. It is also important to explore how limited understanding and skewed ways of thinking hinder the interpreter's ability to grasp fully all the implications and truths that God has made known to humanity through Scripture. Alexander notes there is a deconstructive element to the interpretation of the Bible, especially problematic texts that require what scholars of hermeneutics refer to as "unreading the text." By unreading the text, the interpreter recognizes the presence and layers of violence, misogyny, and oppression engrained in these texts. There is also a constructive element to Alexander's hermeneutic. She insists that interpreters should choose not to normalize violence and oppression in current interpretive efforts. Instead readers should employ interpretations that can serve as correctives and guides for the world and church today.

Chart 6: Alexander's Socio-Political Hermeneutic

Deconstructive Hermeneutics	Step One—Explore ways the text supports or supported injustice, oppression, and capitulation to the ethos of the day and in turn were interpretations that were non-liberating, non-redemptive, and non-prophetic.
	Step Two—Identify ways the text in question is liberating, redemptive, and prophetic.
	Step 3—Find ways to develop theological lessons and practices from both the liberating and non-liberating texts and interpretations of texts, which require a shift from deconstructive to constructive hermeneutics.
Constructive Hermeneutics	Step One—Employ a hermeneutic of recovery instead of discarding or silencing portions of Scripture that appear to represent non-liberating and non-redemptive ways of being in the world.
	Step Two—Privilege social justice implications in Scripture.
	Step Three—Wrestle authentically with problem passages by considering and critiquing the ways the text has been used to buttress oppression. It requires honesty about human failure and limitedness in the text, and taking corporate and personal sins seriously.
	Step Four—Loo for healing, holistic, and liberating aspects in the text.

Alexander's model has also proven to be a helpful way to read and study passages that are problematic in an honest and critical manner that serves the church's broader goal of giving witness to a loving, holy, just, and caring Creator. More importantly, this model has provided a way of correcting the popular and theologically reckless practice of ignoring or discarding passages we may not like. Instead, Alexander's approach provides a way to organize and prioritize texts (with a clear theological picture in mind), a practice I call "rightly dividing" the Scriptures. Paul's instructions to Timothy are helpful reminders of the goal in the interpretation of the Bible:

> Study to shew thyself approved unto God, a workman that needeth not to be ashamed, rightly dividing the word of truth. (2 Tim 2:15 KJV)

Rightly dividing the word of truth means learning how to grapple with the whole of Scripture and its problematic parts in a way that can make theological sense of this multi-volume book believed to be sacred by many Christians. Rightly dividing the word of truth means learning to balance the whole—the Gospel and its parts— with the matrix of stories collected in the canon.

We can be honest about genocide, slavery, and the oppression of women in the Bible. We can also hold to the Bible as the sacred and authoritative text for the Christian church. How? We can do this because there is a big picture—a forward movement, or a core message—that can be discerned in the Bible and that represents what it is all about. We can learn how to hold in tension problematic passages in the Bible with what I identify as the "core message" of the Bible. This is a hermeneutical move that strives to make theological sense of conflicting and problematic texts.

The Core Message of the Bible
Versus Problematic Texts

The "core message" of the Bible includes the major ideas, teachings, and underlying themes that drive the story of God and humanity. The core theological message forms the backdrop against which we are to understand the relation of stories in ancient Israel through to the Greco-Roman period that witnessed the birth of the Jesus movement. It is the thread of thought running throughout Scripture. The core message of the Bible can be discerned through stories and teachings both explicit and implicit. It asks the deeper and larger questions of the Bible: How is God revealed and understood? What has God done in history? What is God doing in the present? What will God do in the future? What are the complex and diverse ways God interacts with nations, communities, and individuals? A "core theological message" keeps the big picture in mind and brings balance and correction to individual and corporate statements that are troubling. Discerning the core theological message prevents readers from having to discard the entire Bible because it contains some problematic passages and teachings.

Chart 7: The Core Theological Message of Bible

Teaching	Sample Texts
1. God is love and the Holy One's primary posture is bent toward humanity, which is rooted in love. God loves all humanity.	Exodus story; John 3:16; 1 John 4:7–12.
2. God instructs, guides, and cares for all persons. God gives commands and laws in order for humans to follow them so that they can experience life to the fullest and in order to prevent humans from harming themselves, others, and creation.	The story of first sin in Gen 2–3; The story of the Ten Commandments in Exod 20, and even the Sermon on the Mount in Matt 5–7.
3. God does not approve of all human action. God is not pleased when humans disobey or break commands given them.	Four sin stories in Gen 4–11; Covenant warnings about unfaithfulness in Deuteronomy; Hosea, Amos and Isaiah contain stories of God's displeasure with injustice and idolatry; John 3:16–19.
4. God makes special covenants and has special relationships with certain people to advance God's purposes and plans for creation. God chooses to enter into special relationships to reveal Godself to persons and the world.	Genesis 12:1–3 and Exodus through Deuteronomy is a major story of God entering into a covenant with the children of Israel; Acts 2 and the book of Hebrews discuss a new covenant with those who believe in Jesus.

5. God is gracious and forgiving when commands and laws are broken. God understands the imperfect and sinful nature of humans, sometimes punishing them for sin or allowing the effects of their decisions to run their course. God also shows mercy and grace for disobedient and rebellious humanity.

God makes accommodations for human sin in many of the stories about sin such as Gen 4–11; Exod 34 and Leviticus talk about forgiveness and atonement; Gospels all view the death of Jesus as an act of divine forgiveness.

6. God is unorthodox and unpredictable—chooses younger siblings and outsiders, for instance. God blesses people who are rejected and fail. God flits scripts, judging when others think God should forgive, and forgiving when others think God should judge.

Story of Achan in Josh 7. Story of David's sin in 2 Sam 11–12. Story of Jonah. Story of Jesus.

7. God does things and allows things that are difficult to understand, accept, and explain. Human freedom is respected by the Holy One in ways that raise questions about the justice of and goodness of God.

Story of Job, Story of the exile in 2 Kings and Dan 1, book of Habakkuk.

8. God is moving creation to a better end, the absence of evil, suffering, and death. Jesus Christ is the primary means through which this will happen.

Passages in the book of Revelation.

This core message gives a more overarching "theological" context for those individual passages that are problematic, attempting to reflect what the Bible is all about when interpreting passages. I am admittedly making an intentional "hermeneutical" decision to keep the big picture in mind as we attempt to interpret individual problematic texts. I believe the core message of the Bible is not about killing people, holding slaves, oppressing women, and justifying wars. It is about a loving God who created the world and all persons in God's image. It is about the one God who works with all persons who are sinful and thoroughly imperfect. God works with people in complex and sometimes mysterious ways so that good triumphs over evil.

This core message is best understood and historically revealed in the life and death of Jesus the Christ, who Christians confess reveals God to the world. In fact, I would maintain that the core theological message of the Bible is consistent with both the life and teachings of Jesus. Jesus adds an additional layer of protection from overly sujective approaches. That is, the core theological message upholds the most important test or standard, namely the "gospel" test.

Chart 8:
The Core Theological Message of Bible and Jesus Christ

Teaching	Sample Verses	Core Message and the Gospel of Jesus Christ	Teachings of Jesus
1. God is love and the Holy One's primary posture is bent toward humanity, which is rooted in love. God loves all humanity.	Exodus story; John 3:16; 1 John 4:7–12.	Jesus placed love as the motivating factor for his coming into the world and love as the reason for him giving himself on the cross.	John 13 and 15
2. God instructs, guides, and cares for all persons. God gives commands and laws in order for humans to follow them so that they can experience life to the fullest and in order to prevent humans from harming themselves, others, and creation.	The story of first sin in Gen 2–3; The story of the Ten Commandments in Exod 20, and even the Sermon on the Mount in Matth 5–7.	Jesus taught his disciples and others about the kingdom of God.	Matt 5–7

3. God does not approve of all human action. God is not pleased when humans disobey or break commands given them.	Four sin stories in Gen 4–11; Covenant warnings about unfaithfulness in Deuteronomy; Hosea, Amos and Isaiah contain stories of God's displeasure with injustice and idolatry; John 3:16–19.	Jesus rebuked his disciples, religious leaders, and other erroneous people.	Matt 11 and 23; Mark 8
4. God makes special covenants and has special relationships with certain people to advance God's purposes and plans for creation. God chooses to enter into special relationships to reveal Godself to persons and the world.	Genesis 12:1–3 and Exodus through Deuteronomy is a major story of God entering into a covenant with the children of Israel; Acts 2 and the book of Hebrews discuss a new covenant with those who believe in Jesus.	Jesus chose disciples, showing them things others were not privy to. Jesus also had individual conversations with persons to whom he revealed mysteries of the kingdom.	Matt 10 and Mark 4
5. God is gracious and forgiving when commands and laws are broken. God understands the imperfect and sinful nature of humans, sometimes punishing them for sin or allowing the effects of their decisions to run their course. God also shows mercy and grace for disobedient and rebellious humanity.	God makes accommodations for human sin in many of the stories about sin such as Gen 4–11; Exod 34 and Leviticus talk about forgiveness and atonement; Gospels all view the death of Jesus as an act of divine forgiveness.	Jesus taught and practiced a radical form of forgiveness.	Matt 18 and John 8 and Luke 23

66

6. God is unorthodox and unpredictable—chooses younger siblings and outsiders, for instance. God blesses people who are rejected and fail. God flits scripts, judging when others think God should forgive, and forgiving when others think God should judge.	Story of Achan in Josh 7. Story of David's sin in 2 Sam 11–12. Story of Jonah. Story of Jesus.	Jesus did many unorthodox things like eating with sinners, talking in public with women, eating with tax collectors, and even turning away women and others who sought him.	Luke 15 and 19, John 4 and 6; Matt 13 and 15
7. God does things and allows things that are difficult to understand, accept, and explain. Human freedom is respected by the Holy One in ways that raise questions about the justice of and goodness of God.	Story of Job, story of the exile in 2 Kings and Dan 1, book of Habakkuk.	Jesus allowed Judas to steal from the bag and ultimately betray him, even though Jesus claimed to know all along he would be betrayed by a disciple.	John 6
8. God is moving creation to a better end, the absence of evil, suffering, and death. Jesus Christ is the primary means through which this will happen.	Passages in the book of Revelation.	Jesus saw himself as chosen by God the Father to save the world from sin and manifest the kingdom of God in its fullness. He will also provide a place of rest for the righteous.	Matt 24 and John 14

It is this understanding of the core message of the Bible that is crucial when dealing with problematic texts like those instructing slaves to obey their earthly masters as they obey Christ, or others teaching that men bear the image and glory of God while women bear the glory of men.

The purpose of discerning and utilizing the core theological message of the Bible is that it provides textual and moral justification to say NO to certain texts—NO to killing in the name of God or religion; NO to silencing women; NO to excluding women from preaching; NO to instructing slaves to obey masters; NO to genocide; NO to condemning divorced persons to hell, etc. Understanding and lifting up what is central in the Bible helps us not to ascribe authority to oppressive texts. It is the ultimate act of faith and reverence to read and interpret the text with care and a disposition to interpretations that are just, compassionate, and loving, as Christ was just, compassionate, and loving.

Using Problematic Texts
to Expose the Dark Side of Religion

Maybe the most important reason for wrestling with problematic texts and not discarding them is that they teach us powerful lessons about a subject many would avoid altogether. Religion is both a tremendous source of good and evil. Humans do great things in the name of religion. They also do horrible things in the name of religion. Religion can inspire self-sacrifice and murder. The dark side of religion means doing harm and evil in the name of God; no religion is exempt, including Christianity. Though I do not agree with him on many matters, the work of John Shelby Spong highlighting the sins of Scripture is important in bringing to light the history of violence and oppression linked to texts in the Bible.[3] People have done evil things in the name of God and used the Bible to justify their actions. Sometimes in our haste to defend God and the Bible, we push aside this issue and ignore the centuries of

---

3. See especially Spong, *Sins of Scripture*.

pain caused by many of the forebearers of our religion. In doing this, we also fail to recognize the perverse logic in our own times that "if they can do it, we can too."

Whatever else we believe it to be, the Bible is certainly an historical document providing an honest account of religious persons and communities—the good, the bad, and the ugly. But for a people of faith, the Bible is also a religious text that many look to for guidance. I fear, however, the uncritical acceptance of *all* texts and the ignorance their history. The truth is that the Bible can be dangerous. Mieke Bal agrees, saying, "The Bible, of all books, is the most dangerous one, the one that has been endowed with the power to kill."[4] Many atheists and agnostics claim that religion have been the most powerful forces for evil. A large part of the force behind the Christian religion is the Bible. The fact is the Bible can be just as dangerous today as it has been in the past, and it is important to admit this.

One of my favorite movies, *The Book of Eli*, starring Denzel Washington and Gary Oldman, illustrates the incredible power of the Bible in society and in the hands of people corrupted by power. In one scene, Eli (Washington) and Carnegie (Oldman) have a showdown of sorts, with Carnegie revealing that he wants the book that audiences will learn later learn is the last copy of the King James Bible on earth.

> (Carnegie says) Look I need that book. I mean, I want that book. And you, if you make me choose I'll kill you. I'll take the book. Why, why do you want it? (Eli asks and Carnegie responds) I grew up with it. I know its power. If you read it, then so do you. That's why they burned it after the war. Just staying alive is an act of faith. Building this town is an even bigger act of faith. But they don't understand. None of them. And I don't have the right words to help them, but the book does. Now I admit I've had to do things, many things to build this. I confess that. But if we had that book I wouldn't have to. Now imagine, imagine how different and how righteous this little world could be if we had the right words for our faith. If people

4. Bal, *Anti-Covenant*, 14.

would truly understand why they're here and why they're doing it, they wouldn't need any of the other ugly motivations. It's not right to keep that book anyway. It's meant to be shared with others. It's meant to be spread.[5]

In the following scene, an injured Carnegie tends to his wound as he instructs his henchmen to prepare to chase Eli. His right-hand man, Redridge (played Ray Stevenson), jested, "for a book?" He was met with Carnegie's response that reveals his deeper, wicked intentions.

> It's not a f---ing book. It's a weapon. A weapon aimed right at the hearts and minds of the weak and the desperate. It will give us control of them. If we want to rule more than this small town, then we have to have it. People will come from all over. They'll do exactly what I'll tell them if the words are from the book. It's happened before. It'll happen again.[6]

He called the book a weapon and was willing to kill to get his hands on it. I know this is only a fictional story but, in many respects, it is a product of the western religious imagination and its history of religiously inspired violence and control. Carnegie knew the power of the Bible as a tool that could be used to shape society and control people. He knew what the slave masters of antebellum America knew. My ancestors dealt with the same thing.

Africans in America were introduced to the Bible by white "Christians" who claimed to worship God yet supported and benefitted from the enslavement of fellow humans. These Christians believed the Bible was central to the life of the church, and many believed it permitted slavery. For a long period of time, white slave owners went to great lengths to keep the Bible away from enslaved Africans for fear that they might read the Bible and thus they would be difficult to control. Over time enslaved people were exposed to Presbyterian, Methodist, and Baptist church traditions. They began to recognize how important it was to shape one's

5. Hughes and Hughes, *Book of Eli.*
6. Hughes and Hughes, *Book of Eli.*

religious identity through Scripture. Enslaved Africans began to interpret Scripture freely, leading to alternate, sometimes revolutionary interpretations and conclusions. Many slave revolts were led by leaders who had read Scripture and acted upon their understanding. This caused slaveholders to believe that "unsupervised reading of the Bible among slaves turned religion into rebellion."[7] They recognized what Carnegie knew in the movie *The Book of Eli*, that the Bible is a powerful tool. So, what they did was commission white missionaries and preachers "to take the teeth out of Evangelical religion."[8] This was done to better control not only enslaved people's bodies but also their minds. Enslavers also reinforced the early anti-literacy laws that ensured the Bible would become a closed book in a religion built around it. In a cruel irony, enslaved Africans hid from professing Christians in order to read the Bible.

A primary purposes of this book is to help students of the Bible to understand that good interpretation is not as easy as reading a verse and saying, "ok I have to do this because it is in the Bible." Good interpretation may recognize that there are texts we should not act on. Good interpretation engages the destructive implicatons of these texts and their interpretive traditions. Good interrpetation requires more than simply ignoring or explaining away these problematic texts and their interpretations. In her influential book, *Texts of Terror,* Phyllis Trible cautions readers against explaining away such texts in unhealthy ways. Any attempt to claim that such texts are relics of a distant and inferior past or that the God of the Old Testament is a God of wrath while the God of the New Testament is a God of love is inadequate. Trible rejects attempts to subordinate suffering to the suffering of Jesus on the cross or the attempt to redeem such suffering in light of the resurrection. She challenges readers to sit with these texts because "sad stories do not have happy endings."[9] So then, what is the purpose of such texts being included in the Bible? How are they useful for "instruction in righteousness," to use the language

---

7. Callahan, *Talking Book*, 9.

8. Callahan, *Talking Book*, 9.

9. Trible, *Texts of Terror,* 2.

of 2 Tim 3:16–17? Trible argues the problematic texts in the Bible function as a mirror of the painful realities of a sinful world. As art imitates life, Scripture likewise reflects both holiness and horror. Reflections themselves neither mandate nor manufacture change, yet by enabling insight, they inspire repentance. In other words, sad stories may yield new beginnings.[10]

Problematic texts illustrate the contradictions and evils we face in life today. That is why problematic texts can be an interpretive gift to the church. Problematic texts are sober warnings of practices and actions to be avoided and corrected, not emulated. These texts warn us of the dangers of using them to justify violence and/or oppression of some kind. The inclusion of these texts is meant to teach us about the pervasive dangers of faith communities weaving violence and oppression into the fabric of our worship, the construction of our communities, and our multidirectional relationship between God and each other (love God and love neighbor in Luke 10; love God by loving neighbor in 1 John 4).

In the book *Does the Bible Justify Violence*, John Collins makes a similarly compelling point. He echoes Trible in that problematic texts reflect realities of imperfect persons and communities. He writes, "The power of the Bible is largely that it gives an unvarnished picture of human nature and the dynamics of history, and also of religion and the things that people do in its name."[11] Although there may be embarrassing aspects for religious persons and communities who do not like their dirty laundry aired before the world, there is a benefit in biblical stories and texts telling the full truth about themselves. It makes the clear and strong point that even religious persons and communities are imperfect, do harmful things, and often attempt to justify such things using the name of God. But Collins goes on to emphasize the problem of misunderstanding why such texts are included in the canon of Scripture in the first place.

10. Trible, *Texts of Terror*, 2.
11. Collins, *Does the Bible Justify Violence?* 31.

> The biblical portrayal of human reality becomes perni-
> cious only when it is vested with authority and assumed
> to reflect, without qualification or differentiation, the
> wisdom and or will of God ... neither does it claim that
> the stories it tells are paradigms for human action in all
> times and places.[12]

Problematic texts are not meant to be used as paradigms for human action; we are not meant to repeat harmful and deadly actions. These texts found their way into the canon for broader instructive purposes. There is wisdom in including problematic texts in Scripture. They cut to deep issues about humans and faith communities in unique and impactful ways. Editing or removing these texts would provide a sterile and unrealistic picture of human life that could not address issues like ethnic killing, patriarchy, and the grotesque ways humans structure society around class. These texts are included in the canon of Scripture not to encourage such behavior but rather to expose our tendency to do evil in the name of God and faith. In some respects, we may have missed the wisdom Scripture has tried to impart. Instead of recognizing mistakes not to repeat, we emulate the very practices connected to a history that did not end well. It is my hope that church leaders, preachers, and teachers will learn these valuable "hermeneutical" lessons that Scripture is trying to teach us.

---

12. Collins, *Does the Bible Justify Violence?* 31.

Part Two

From the Text to Our Context

Chapter Five

The Bible and Incarnational Truth

LEARNING TO INTERPRET THE Bible this way is ultimately an act of faith in God, not in the Bible itself. For too long, conservative churches have elevated the Bible, which is the product of divine inspiration and activity, over the producer: God. Too often we forget about God and God's intentions, often referred to as "divine will." We lose sight of the wondrous and mysterious ways God uses texts in Scripture to form, guide, strengthen, and instruct us. After all, Scripture is a guide in righteousness; it is a text that ever calls us to look to the Holy One. Faithful interpretation is interpretation that first "lifts our eyes to the hills from whence comes our help (Ps 121:1). In the spirit of the Paraclete passages in John 14–16, anything birthed by the Holy Spirit, including the writings of Scripture, should point not to itself but to Jesus. One of the surest signs that contemporary interpretations have erred from the Spirit of God is the dogmatic insistence on looking to the book and relegating God to a secondary status. The Spirit in Scripture calls our gaze to God and God's Son. It is only by looking up and turning to Jesus that we see the words of Scripture rightly and use them rightly to build a better church and a better world.

Looking at Scripture Differently

Linda MacCammon talks about the role of faith and viewing Scripture differently in her book *Liberating the Bible*. She confesses, "Faith is about trust in God's intentions for the world and in God's promises as revealed in the many gifts offered throughout the biblical story and throughout our own lives. Thus, we have a grasp of the whole if we are to make any sense of the individual parts." Her understanding of the whole is revealing.

> [T]he governance structure and pedagogical program Yahweh develops in Genesis and Exodus, refines in Isaiah, and extends in the New Testament are canonical, that is, they function together as an authoritative paradigm or model of faith communities to construct their own ethics and morality. In crafting the program—which holds the polarities of faith and doubt, virtue and duty, love and justice, mystery and certainty, and tradition and innovation in creative tension and balance—God's intention is not to produce unreflective rule-followers who parrot the dictates of a divine-command morality. On the contrary, God's strategy is designed to transform readers of the Bible into God-fearing servants of the creation who think critically about their faith, who are open to innovation, change, and doubt, and who have the ability to construct moralities that uphold justice and foster peace for their own time and place. Thus, contrary to the rulebook model espoused by many Christians, the Bible is best understood as a revelatory text that illuminates rather than legislates.[1]

In her own way, MacCammon insists on the importance of recognizing the "core theological message" as the key to knowing how to understand the varying parts and messages in the writings of the Bible. As I've repeatedly empasized, it is critical to recognize the core theological message of the Bible and its overarching theological framework instead of attempting to systematize every verse. I believe this to be an honest approach to problematic texts

---

1. MacCammon, *Liberating the Bible*, 245–46.

while holding fast to the Bible. I hope this provides a way for readers to wrestle with this important theological issue.

The Importance of the Incarnation

All of the preceding would suggest, then, that there is an incarnational dimension to the importance of recognizing the core theological message of the Bible. The doctrine of the incarnation is a Christian concept that claims 2,000 years ago God became flesh in the person of Jesus Christ. The New Testament idea that the *Logos* represented the divine revelation of God in the person of Jesus Christ is taught in the Gospel of John. The logos is often translated as the "Word," the translation I will use going forward. In the opening chapter, the Gospel of John describes how the eternal word came in human flesh:

> In the beginning was the Word, and the Word was with God, and the Word was God. He was with God in the beginning. Through him all things were made; without him nothing was made that has been made. In him was life, and that life was the light of all mankind. The light shines in the darkness, and the darkness has not overcome it . . . He came to that which was his own, but his own did not receive him . . . . The Word became flesh and made his dwelling among us. We have seen his glory, the glory of the one and only Son, who came from the Father, full of grace and truth. (John 1:1–5, 11, 14)

The incarnation shows how God takes that which is weak and frail, human flesh, to house that which is strong and eternal, the word, in such a way that what is human can be so full of the divine that it impacts people and the world in a transformational manner. Incarnation shows the power of God over material flesh and the presence of God in material flesh, which is why it is such an important doctrine.

John's description of the incarnation teaches four things important for our understanding of the incarnational nature of truth: (1) Jesus was eternal; (2) Jesus took on human flesh; (3) the world was in darkness, which often implied a lack of understanding of divinely revealed truth; and (4) human beings often did not receive the logos, but those who did became sons and daughters of God. These four elements occur throughout John's Gospel. Jesus also makes "I am" statements throughout John's Gospel (6:35; 8:12; 10:7, 11, 14; 11:25; 14:6; 15:1, and esp. 8:58). John 1 climaxes with the claim that the word became "flesh" and dwelt among us (1:14).

However, the latter two aspects of John's understanding are particularly important, both for how they played out in the life of Jesus and also for what they mean for succeeding generations of persons grappling with eternal truth that is incarnational in nature. New Testament scholar Raymond Brown documents two motifs that are pertinent here. John uses misunderstanding and double meaning to illustrate the difficulties people had understanding the eternal word that took on human flesh.

> Although he comes from above and speaks what is "true" or real (heavenly reality), Jesus, the Word become flesh, must use language from below to convey his message. To deal with this anomaly, he frequently employs figurative language or metaphors to describe himself or to present his message (2:19–21; 3:3–4; 4:10–11; 6:26–27; 8:33–35; 11:11–13). In an ensuing dialogue the questioner will misunderstand the figure or metaphor, and take only a material meaning. This allows Jesus to explain his thought more thoroughly and thereby to unfold his doctrine.[2]

> Sometimes playing into misunderstanding, sometimes simply showing the multifaceted aspect of revelation, a double meaning often can be found in what Jesus says. (a) There are plays on various meanings of a given word that Jesus uses, meanings based on either Hebrew or Greek; sometimes the dialogue partner may take one meaning, while Jesus intends the other. ("lifted up" in 3:14; 8:28; 12:34- crucifixion and return to God; "living water" in 4:10- flowing water and life giving water; "die for" instead or on behalf of. (b) The author frequently

2. Brown, *Introduction to the New Testament*, 333–34.

intends the reader to see several layers of meaning in the same narrative or in the same metaphor.[3]

It is a marvelous thing to consider the eternal God taking on human flesh and using human words and concepts to describe truths that surpass human understanding—experiencing rebirth, renewal, communion, and love. His words were often misunderstood and sometimes completely rejected. Nicodemus thought Jesus meant a literal rebirth. The woman at the well did not understand worship. Many disciples did not understand the depth of communion that Jesus invited his disciples to experience, thinking he was teaching a form of cannibalism. For them, the problem was with literalism, particularly for some of the religious leaders. They were mired in the literal, in the exact nature of a law or a statement or a tradition. Yet, other times the problem was deeper. Some persons could not see the truth even as Jesus attempted to explain it because their hearts and minds were closed to a deeper understanding of divine truth. They believed themselves to have already had sight and understood the truth. As a result, they were left in darkness. Jesus said,

> "For judgment I have come into this world, so that the blind will see and those who see will become blind." Some Pharisees who were with him heard him say this and asked, "What? Are we blind too?" Jesus said, "If you were blind, you would not be guilty of sin; but now that you claim you can see, your guilt remains. (John 9:39–41)

Later in John, some of these persons were eventual participants in the betrayal and execution of the eternal word.

Incarnation and Truth

What John described in the life of Jesus is instructive for the church today and the interpretation of Scripture. Historically, when scholars and theologians talked about the incarnation, much of the focus was on the relation between his divine and human nature.

3. Brown, *Introduction to the New Testament*, 335.

They struggled to understand how an eternal being could reside in a temporal body. Christian theologians debated the complexities of the eternal God who had no limitations but dwelled in a human body that had limitations. Jesus was hungry, thirsty, tired, and died while never ceasing to be God. This is not a new conversation among Christians. Early debates in the church, like Arianism for example, centered on the issue of the nature of Jesus.

However, incarnation has another implication for theology. The incarnation of Jesus teaches us about truth itself. If truth is the product of the revelatory work of God, it has to have an incarnational component and work in a similar way as truth worked in the life of Jesus. The eternal and worldly become the context for revelation. That is how it worked for Jesus. That is how it works today. Incarnational truth is a helpful way to frame the conflict we are all invited into when a perfect God uses imperfect things for the revelation of truth. Just as Jesus was the eternal word in John's Gospel, so, too, does eternal truth exist in an imperfect world, particularly in a text with problematic statements. Interestingly, conservatives, liberals, and even non-Christians agree on that. Yet, I maintain, this incarnational way of understanding truth is a model for hermeneutics that informs my work and my insistence on the importance of discerning the core theological message of the Bible.

Misunderstanding, on the one hand, and double, sometimes deeper, meanings, on the other hand, are recurring motifs about Jesus in the Gospel of John. These motifs are similar to problems people have today when it comes to discerning the eternal message in the Bible. Some people are stuck in a kind of literalism that restates specific commands no matter how problematic they may be. Others may be stuck in a literalism that believes the Bible cannot speak truth in a way that reflects the reality of God and the gospel because a particular text is problematic. Both are understandable responses. It is not easy to peer beyond the literal and the problematic to see the eternal as best we can. However, it is more possible to do so with aids like the Holy Spirit and faithful, thoughtful, learned teachers. After all, Jesus promised that the Holy Spirit, not the Bible, would guide us into all truth (John 16:13). John's Gospel warns about the dangers of blind and rigid literalism and its accompanying systems of thought. Instead of bringing us into the light, they often leave us in the dark and make us unable to see God standing right in front of us. If you do not believe me, ask Pontius Pilate, who stood in front of God in the flesh and retorted, "What is truth?" (John 18:38). He had no idea who stood before him.

Truth has to be incarnational—eternal and worldly, perfect and imperfect. This explains why the dual doctrines of the inerrancy and infallibility of the Bible are foolish and wrongheaded, because they distort the incarnational nature of truth.[4] These mistaken doctrines try to ascribe a level of perfection to the biblical text reserved only for God. This erroneous line of thinking leads theologians, pastors, and leaders into making intellectually dishonest statements, such as the Bible in its original and first forms is inerrant and infallible. The problem with this logic is that we do not possess the original and first forms of the text. We have copies of copies, and, for a large number of the writings, we are not exactly sure who originally wrote them. We just know they were written and passed down and became incredibly important to ancient communities. All this energy invested in fighting for a perfect text detracts from our worship and faith in a perfect God who knows how to use imperfection to communicate truth. God can use vessels with flaws. God does it all the time with preachers and teachers. I have been preaching for 30 years; I know firsthand that God knows how to work with what is imperfect to accomplish divine purposes. In the same way God uses imperfect preachers to proclaim truth, God can use a text with problematic statements to reveal divine will and guide people in matters of faith.

The incarnational nature of truth challenges also critics of a sacred text containing problematic statements. Humanistic and atheistic critics of the Bible cannot accept an imperfect text like

4. See Angela Parker's compelling assessment of the doctrine of inerrancy as an expression of white supremacist authoritarianism in *If God Still Breathes Why Can't I?*

the Bible either. Admittedly, there is no excusing some of the statements contained in the Bible and the harmful ways these texts have been used to victimize and kill people. There is no cleaning up the history or fixing the myriad of problems associated with these texts. They are problematic and wrongheaded. However, it does not mean the Bible cannot be revelatory and special in a way that surpasses all other texts. Christians believe the Bible is sacred—not because it is perfect or without problems, but because it is the vehicle God has chosen to reveal Godself to the world. God chose imperfect people and the messiness of their lives and communities to reveal Godself. It is messy and beautiful and mysterious.

This idea that the biblical text itself is not perfect is a difficult concept for some to grasp. However, I believe, it is a liberating truth that better grounds hermeneutics in worship of the true God. It is liberating for three reasons. First, it reminds us of the foundational doctrine of the worship of God. Only God is perfect, and to ascribe perfection to things crafted by human hands is idolatrous. Second, it reminds us of God's power. God is powerful enough to use problematic and imperfect interpreters; to claim otherwise, displays a level of pride that is idolatrous. Third, it gives us space for subjectivity in interpretation because interpretation itself is a spiritual and communal act. Yes, our discernment of God's work is subjective and messy and imperfect; it does not answer all the questions nor solve all the problems. That is fine. God works with us through the Spirit, and God works in communities that desire to be faithful to the word. God helps us to discern truth through the careful study of Scripture. It is still important to read and study the Bible! The point of emphasis is the subject of interpretation, namely God, the one who joins the readers in interpretation and helps them flesh out meaning in ways that are true to the message of truth imbedded in the text.

The perfect God—not the text—utilizes imperfect people, tools, words, cultures, and writings to reveal truth to the world. The Bible gives evidence of God's ability to do this and is itself a product of his incarnational work in history. Our task in interpretation, then, is to discern the kernel of the eternal in the hull of the temporal. This is what I have attempted to do with the whole of Scripture. It can also be applied to individual problematic texts. Take for example the story of a centurion soldier in Matt 8. It is a problematic text because it deals with the relationship between a master and his slave. Important truths nonetheless exist in the story, such as the care for the sick and vulnerable, as well as the faith in God's power to heal. These form the kernel—the core truths—in the story. But is problematic that they are surrounded by a hull that seems to legitimize societal ideas built on the enslavement and domination of other people. The centurion is a slave master and as such exercises a level of control and unquestioned compliance that he brags about in the story: "I tell them to go. I tell them to come." These statements are the hull, the problematic parts we should not normalize and condone.

This approach teaches us an important aspect of the meaning of "rightly dividing the word of truth," which means knowing the part of a story to emulate and the part not to. "Rightly dividing the word of truth" also means understanding that God uses human ideas, words, and systems rooted in sinful cultures to reveal truth. It is important to discern the truth in a text without making sacred the imperfections necessary for eternal ideas to enter the world. So, when interpreting this story in Matt 8, our task is both to embrace the model to follow the care shown for the vulnerable, and also to critique the ways in which systems are built in the world that leave people to be dominated in this way. This additional interpretive layer requires giving more thought to the meaning and application of the text for today. It is not an easy task but one we are called to do nonetheless. In the end, it is possible that the greatest gift problematic texts give us is a bigger vision of God and a sobering vision of the word. I hope readers will leave Matt 8 with these dual hermeneutical gifts because it is only then that we can rightly divide the word of truth.

Chapter Six

Collateral Damage and the Bible

I AM SURE YOU have heard of the concept of collateral damage. It is often used in popular action movies by villains willing to harm innocent lives in a sadistic plot. They claim something like, "Anytime two powerful forces clash, there will be collateral damage." Collateral damage refers to unintended but real harm experienced by those on the periphery of situations. In military action, collateral damage refers to an incidental death or wound of a non-combatant. The concept of collateral damage reminds us that in life people can be killed or severely wounded in a conflict that does not directly involve them.

While you may know about this concept, I am fairly certain you have not heard it connected to the interpretation of the Bible. I believe, however, that the concept of collateral damage has import for how we read and interpret the Bible. We read the Bible to understand who God is and how to live faithfully in response to the Holy One's claim on our lives. To use the language of 2 Tim 3:16–17, Scripture is inspired by God and is profitable for instruction in righteousness. As we read stories and study passages, the expectation is learning something that will improve our lives both before God and how we relate to others. However, we do not read the Bible unfiltered; we interpret it even at the most basic reading level because it has been translated from ancient languages, originates from ancient cultures, utilizes ancient literary devices and genres

86

that affect meaning, contains highly problematic teachings and stories, and has been handed down by others for centuries. Interpretation requires great care in any attempt to extrapolate meaning from the Bible for life today. Engaging the Bible for meaning and truth for our lives today requires both reading and interpretation.

Victims in the Bible

If you read and study Scripture with care and attention to detail, you will find stories of people victimized by others and sometimes by God. The Bible contains stories of victims caught up in situations not of their own making. There are stories of lives lost in clashes between nations, families, individuals, and even divine forces and beings. In these clashes, people directly involved in wrongdoing are often punished and sometimes die. But, there are others who suffer and die and are not involved in conflict or wrongdoing. I refer to these people as the *"silent characters of the Bible"* because they are often ignored and overlooked when we read stories in the Bible. We focus too much on the main characters, too often overlooking these silent characters and their stories of suffering. These silent characters in the Bible are important, too. Their stories matter. There are texts in the Bible that suggest God cares about smaller, silent characters. For exanple, one Gospel writer records Jesus mentioning that God numbers the hairs on our heads (Matthew 10:30). That is a small matter for an all-wise and all-powerful God to know. There are stories of Jesus giving attention to unspoken thoughts (Matt 9:4; Luke 11:17), which indicates the important of the silent matters. Jesus even suggests in Matthew that every idle word spoken will be accounted for by God (12:36–37). If small things matter to God, they should matter to us as well. This would seem to suggest that some things we think are trivial are actually important.

The stories of these silence victims in the Bible are neither subjects nor objects of sermons or studies. Their experiences and perspectives do not inform our theology. Preachers and theologians alike do not find these stories instructive and important for our reflection and understanding of the meaning of suffering, loss, and sometimes death. I believe that our refusal to engage these stories is why, at times, both our preaching and theology lack existential depth and fail to connect with people who experience the underside of life. It is not an uncommen criticisms of churches that they are irrelevant. I have spent years interrogating this claim and trying to understand what fuels this belief today. What I have found are people who experience a disconnect between what they see in the world and what they they hear about the world from preachers' sermons. Congrigants and pastors alike have trouble relating and connecting to the broad gamut of human experience. Our inability to connect hermeneutically with all people in the Scriptures hinders our ability to do so in preaching, theology, and everyday life.

Our theology possesses an inescapable contradiction. On one hand we claim that all life is sacred and valuable. We believe that every person is created in the image of God. On the other hand, and in seeming contradiction to the belief that all life is special, ther are beliefs and practices that suggest some lives are more important than others and—even worse!—that some people's lives are expendable. This contradiction is also latent in our approach to stories in the Bible. We worship and revere Jesus for giving his life for others and as a result we teach the principle of agape love that is self-giving and should be shared with others. Yet, our behavior too often demonstrate favoritism and/or mistreatment of others. We read stories both in our sacred texts and secular news in which people are lost or skipped over as if those lives did not matter. I do not mean to raise the death of others to that of Jesus's death, but I do want to highlight how we too easily ignore the lives of others in our rush to place value on a life given as applied to Jesus's life. Do you see the contradiction?

Because we ignore these characters, we also ignore people like them in our world. A few years ago, Black and white churches were trying to figure out what to do about the Black Lives Matter movement and where they stood on this issue. Many did not understand the need to affirm Black Lives Matter in the context of police brutality and injustice in the criminal justice system. Others felt the need to affirm that *all* lives matter. The "all lives matter" claim was well-intended but missed the point altogether, and instead reflected a gross misunderstanding of the historical context that framed the expression Black Lives Matter. One cannot affirm Black Lives Matters while negating the context and meaning of the affirmation with the alternative claim of All Lives Matter. The point in this brief foray is to show that churches were not prepared to enter this conversation, and it hurt the credibility of our witness. Our churches and theological institutions cannot teach laypeople and leaders to believe "Black Lives Matter" or the lives of immigrants or refugees matter because our hermeneutical approach is limited and skewed. Because our focus is often on the main characters, we cannot interpret the Bible and preach in a way that shows all people's lives in the Bible matter. A survey of popular books about the Bible sold in Christian bookstores will not reveal minor characters or those who are victims of social injustices. In these books, men and slave masters matter. Stories of women, the enslaved, children, foreigners, and scores of unnamed people in the Bible do not matter as much. This hermeneutical approach has decided implications for how people and communities are treated.

American Christianity has a history of being callous and ignoring the pain of victims. It has a history of ignoring collateral suffering, some of which is the result of American Christian preachers neglecting these stories in the Bible. Let me give an example of this history. Millions of Africans suffered and died during slavery, which was an American Holocaust that lasted nearly three centuries. During a time when millions of Africans suffered human rights atrocities in the worst ways imaginable, so-called Christian preaching and teaching ignored their suffering. In fact, most expressions of white Christianity were adjusted to the grotesque realities of human enslavement, behavior that forever indicts these churches as unfaithful and sinful expressions of Christian faith. The deeper problem is that we have not corrected the tendency to adjust Christian belief and practice to mass suffering and death. Today, hundreds of people are victims of the new scourge of mass shootings. Thousands of people are dying at the hands of gunmen. Better gun laws and other legislative changes have not occurred because the callous nerves that run deep in this country and its religious institutions prevents us from collectively working to correct the issue. We will express our condolences and move on within a day or two because loss, mass suffering, and death are not that big a deal. Worse yet, we completely ignore all the lives scarred by mass suffering of this kind. Why do we ignore the collateral damage? Why do we fail to hear the silent characters? I worry what future generations of Christians will say about today's Christians when the bill for the suffering and death at the hands of gunmen and a country addicted to violence comes due. Our choice to ignore the collateral damage, the silent characters, the suffering causes us to lose our humanity one day at a time. We need a change, but where do we begin? I believe we begin with the word of God and how we use it to inform teaching and living.

Hermeneutics as a Way to Recapture our Humanity

The journey to recapturing the humanity we've collectively lost by enslaving Africans, exterminating Native Americans, and watching people senselessly die as we worship guns and violence, can be recovered by learning to engage the biblical text at a deeper and more creative level. There is more to good hermeneutics than making proper connections between ancient and modern cultures and language. Good textual interpretation also involves attending to people and stories not always viewed in a normative manner, Too often stories and characters are ignored because of assumptions that they do not contain significant meaning for readers. Attending to this gap is important for modern students of Scripture, including many pastors, who are losing interest in drawing on the hermeneutical insights their reading, teaching, and preaching. More importantly, attending to this gap provides a way to help the church recapture its humanity and deepen its understanding of faith and life in a fallen world—a world that is not what it ought to be.

I hope ministers and theological educators take up the following stories and challenge hearers and students of the sacred text to grapple with their meaning and the manifold lessons they teach. A good place to begin is with the following stories, what we might call the "Victims in the Bible." They can teach us a thing or two about collateral damage and struggle, and thorugh the search for meaning by way of good hermeneutics, they can lead the student of the text to better make sense of the experiences of all the characters in the texts.

1. The women and children of the Amalekites who were commanded to be killed in 1 Sam 15;

2. Uriah the Hittite in 2 Sam 11;

3. The baby born of David and Bathsheba who died in 2 Sam 12;

4. Jephthah's daughter and the other women who grieved with her before her tragic death in Judg 11;

5. Achan's wife and children in Josh 7;

6. The men (we presume) soldiers who died outside the furnace in Dan 3; and

7. Onesimus, the slave who fled the house of his master Philemon.

There are many such stories of collateral damage, including women and children ordered to be executed by a prophet of God for sins they did not commit, women raped and decapitated, and countless soldiers dying in conflicts.[1] These people did nothing wrong. They did not activcle participate in a situation, and yet they suffered in profound ways, sometimes even losing their lives.

Hermeneutics is primarily focused on understanding the original occasion (or meaning) and original language of the text, while secondarily it is concerned with the meaning of the text for readers. When it comes to these stories, I want you to focus on the latter aim. I recommend doing some study to understand the

1. For these stores and others like them, see 1 Samuel 15:1–3; Judges 19:22–30; and the full narratives of Joshua and the two volumes of Kings.

passage and its historical and literary context, but I do not want to get bogged down in this part and fail to grapple with the profound theological and philosophical questions these stories raise for readers and more importantly, the church today. I want to encourage my readers to make two different hermeneutical moves. First, it is important to read these stories and then enter into the existential emotion and complexity these stories are meant to engender in readers. A part of entering into the emotive and deeper philosophical aspects of interpretation is asking questions about what happened to these people. Then readers must grapple with the meaning and implications of these stories at both the theological and philosophical level.

Entering into the text is actually another way the Scriptures renew the mind. God transforms us as we read and internalize the word. By internalizing the word, it helps to recondition, correct, and sensitize our thinking in ways better aligned with the will of God and not the thinking of a sinful world. That is why it is important to enter into the world of the text and the experiences of persons in the text, especially those who experienced collateral suffering.

Asking questions like these is a good place to begin.

1. Why did the person or persons in the story suffer and or die?

2. What is justice in this situation and why does it matter?

3. Where is God in the story?

4. How is God portrayed in the story and what does the text explain as divine action in the story?

5. Is God active or passive in the story?

6. Why include these details in the story, or why is this person's story important in the larger narrative and context?

7. Is there meaning in the suffering and/or death of persons in these stories or are their lives like pawn pieces on a chess board? (Please do not rush to answer this. Think about the question.)

8. Is there hope for these people in this life and/or beyond death?

9. What if this person or people were your spouse, son or daughter, sibling, parent, or close friend?

10. How would your relationship affect your understanding and response to the situation?

11. Would it matter if this were you in the story?

12. Do you want to experience this and why does the question matter?

It is particularly important to wrestle with questions about God's presence and agency in these stories because these are the precise issues that stir doubt, pessimism, and disbelief in some who read these stories and question God's role in pain, violence, suffering, and death. Readers can enter into the existential emotion of the text by placing themselves in and giving interpretive focus to victims. This is a different hermeneutical move rarely taken by interpreters. We too often skip over these people.

It bears special emphasis. Wrestling with divine agency in a story and/or asking pointed questions about God's portrayal in biblical narratives is a difficult task. It can appear to be irreverent. However, it does not have to be, if one is honestly trying to take seriously first the text and second God's care for all persons in creation. Both convictions require an honest assessing of all characters and stories in the Bible. God is all-wise and all-powerful; I am pretty confident that God is not shaken when we deeply engage all the angles, characters, and truths imbedded in the text.

The second hermeneutical move entails drawing some preliminary lessons from these stories that can serve as theological touchstones and points of orientation to guide deeper reflection. Let me demonstrate what this could look like. On the surface, these stories teach sobering truths about the precarious and messy nature of life and the ways these truths intersect with the divine will.

1. The stories of Achan's family and Uriah teach that people can be negatively affected by the actions of others. Both stories seem to suggest it is an inescapable reality, and something we face in our own lives, that harsh circumstances are often the result of the actions of others.

2. The story of Jephthah's daughter shows that God allows human freedom and decisions to run their course, not intervene, even when things go terribly wrong. God's permissive will raises hard questions about a host of issues.

3. The story of Philemon and Onesimus encourage us to be cognizant of the effect of our actions on others. We can turn others away from God and therefore we should try as much as we can to consider the impact of our actions on others, even those too easily deemed unworthy.[2]

These are helpful lessons we can draw from these stories. They can serve as markers and ideas to revisit. However, it is important that our thinking about the meaning of life and the collateral nature of suffering does not end with these lessons. They are only meant to be preliminary. These stories are meant to confound and complicate our understanding of life. Uriah, Achan's wife and children, and the countless Amalekite children executed by the command of a prophet speaking for God all complicate our interpretive tasks becasue they show us a side of life often ignored in popular preaching and teaching. But these stories do more than complicate, they also provide opportunit to deepen our faith and understaning. Our thinking about the text must go beyond cursory statements and trite anecdotes. We have to wade into the deep and trecherous waters of moral ambiguity and stare into the face of nihilism because there are people facing these challenges on a daily basis.

---

2. I encourage you to read Brogdon, *Companion to Philemon*, a book that explains how Philemon's behavior not only hurt Onesimus, his slave, but also was the reason Onesimus was not a Christian.

Hermeneutics as a Way to Wade
into Moral Ambiguity and Nihilism

These stories provide hard lessons about life and faith that require honesty, humility, and accepting truths that are incomprehensible. Life is not fair. Undeserved suffering and death happen all the time. We cannot always understand why; meaning can be elusive. I admit here that this is the most difficult part of the existential and emotive interpretive experience. Stories about collateral damage in the Bible bring readers to the brink of moral chaos and even to the nihilistic belief there is no meaning in the world. The child born of David's rape of Bathsheba is, in essence, killed by God to punish David. Nathan the prophet tells David the child will die but David will be allowed to live. For David, God showed mercy. For this baby, God has not shown mercy but instead prevented him from living for reasons that have nothing to do with him. Surely this qualifies as a problematic text? No one can know why God chooses mercy for one and not another, but there is no escaping the moral difficulty with divine agency in some stories in the Bible. We simply have to wade into such issues and not ignore them.

Sometimes as a reader we reach the limits of human understanding. For example, we may find that we do not have an answer to a "why" question about the suffering of a silent character in a text. That is OK. There are times we are left with the sober realization that "collateral" suffering and sometimes death are inevitable dimensions of life in a fallen and sinful world. We cannot always understand why some people suffer and others do not. This is why the simple statement "life is not fair" is a profound statement about the nature of life. Life is not fair, and who it is who suffers in the world does not always have anything to do with personal choices. We live in a senseless world where the exercise of wisdom does not always guarantee success and peace. Clearly, situations exist in which suffering and death are the result of abusive and sinful ways of exercising human freedom. But that is not always the case. In some stories in the Bible, God is a primary or secondary cause of suffering and death. The point is this: explanations do not have to solve every problem. What they should do is challenge us to explore deeper reflection of faith in the face of moral ambiguity and nihilism. Wrestling with these difficult questions will have decided implications for many pastoral challenges, including the kind of sermons we preach, the kind of questions we ask of the text, the way we approach the task of theology, and our understanding of what it means to be pastoral to those in difficult and despairing situations. Facing these ambiguities is important and healthy because it gives us opportunities to be honest about the limits of human understanding. Preachers and teachers have opportinities to strengtehn and deepen their faith and the faith of their congregations, if they would only use morally ambiguous in thoughtful and creative ways. Pretending that such ambiguities and nihilistic features do not exist only feeds unbelief. They can be features of faith allowing us to differentiate what we know from what we do not know, what we understand from what we do not understand, and what we have come to realize from life experience and study from what continues to baffle and mystify us. Sometimes hermeneutics require the courage to say, "I don't know but I am trying to understand this experience and see its importance."

This second order hermeneutical exercise (focusing on the meaning of the text for us) gives American Christianity a much-needed opportunity to begin the process of recovering our humanity. It begins by seeing those previously invisible and moves to understanding and speaking to the underside of life. Recapturing our humanity is not always having answers to these questions and solutions to the dilemmas and complexities they raise. The point is that we take the time to sit in a different existential space and think about experiences that challenge a deeper understanding and reflection of life. The experience of being treated as chattel or being collateral in a situation not of one's making confronts us with a mis-ordered world with senseless dimensions to it. We do not have to explain it away or justify it. It is what it is. If we really think about it, there has to be a nihilistic or "senseless" dimension to our preaching, for it to be truly theistic and reverent because we are finite beings in relationship with an infinite and eternal God.

We are not supposed to have all the answers. However, we are supposed to ask questions about the stories in the Bible and the experiences of the persons therein. It is a vital part of what it means to be faithful to the witness of God in the world. This is why the issue of collateral damage in the Bible is so important. If handled correctly, these stories are a gift to the church. Instead of collateral suffering resulting in a breakdown of one's faith, it is possible to experience a deepening of faith that sensitizes us to others.

From Hermeneutics to Praxis that Advocates for the Vulnerable

Reading these stories can also prevent us from getting locked into the cycle of inaction in the face of a mis-ordered and unjust world. This can happen. Moral ambiguity and nihilism are responses to a society in which mass suffering and death are commonplace. In the face of the enormity of these things, many choose inaction because they cannot find attainable solutions to end suffering and prevent death. The signs of inaction abound today, and I caution preachers and teachers from ignoring it. A hopelessness pervades today as more people feel nothing can be done in much the same way nothing could be done to help the babies, children, and women we read about in these stories. We must realize that inaction only compounds and exacerbates the dire conditions. Choosing not to speak up and not to try our best to help people who suffer are alternatives we should not consider for a single moment. Surrendering to moral chaos only ensures its permanence and growth.

Reading these stories should not cause us to adopt a passive "bad things happen in the world" kind of stance. Accepting the senseless nature of life can be a gift that prevents us from getting bogged down by suffering and death. There is a third hermeneutical move I want to suggest. On one hand, these stories reveal the rough edges of a world that is not as it should be, yet on another hand, there are other stories that reveal ways of being in the world that can counter or sometimes prevent collateral suffering. Let me explain. Reading and studying certain stories in the Bible should reinforce the important practice of counter-interpretation and reading the whole of Scripture. A community of believers can use another text in the Bible to give a broader meaning and application to the problematic text.

Stories of collateral damage can be held in tension with other stories in which biblical characters model ways to respond to a world where people suffer and die in a needless manner. These stories are important ideological and theological resources for the meaning-making aspects of preaching, teaching and Christian praxis (what it means to live faithfully in the world). Many stories in the Bible model a praxis that advocates for those in vulnerable positions and provides care for them. Let me list four biblical stories that serve as paradigms or models for a praxis that advocates and cares for those experiencing collateral suffering of some kind.

1. The story of Jonah and Ninevites is an example of how mass suffering and death are averted because God chose mercy even though God's prophet wanted judgment and death.

2. The stories of Paul and the wrecked ship in Acts 28 and Paul and Silas in jail at Philippi in Acts 16 are examples of someone preventing others from harming themselves.

3. The letter to Philemon gives a story in which Paul advocates for a slave named Onesimus who likely experienced abuse from his master.

4. Luke 9:49–50 provides a brief account of the twelve disciples' desire to silence other disciples who are not with them. Jesus corrects their misplaced zeal.

In the end, these stories provide models and point ways forward for us in the world—do what we can to prevent both mass and individual suffering and death; advocate for the vulnerable; challenge and correct misplaced religious zeal. These are things we can do. We can daily choose to advocate and care for the vulnerable. This is what I mean by praxis—what we do with what we believe and know. Reading and studying stories of collateral damage should sensitize us to people we have been socialized to ignore.

Adding these other stories to our hermeneutical repertoire gives us practical steps we can join God in the work of doing justice and caring for "the least of these."

Chapter Seven

Reimagining The Bible's Relevance for Today

ONE OF THE GIFTS I hope this book will offer is a different starting point for conversations about God, theology, and faith, and how they intersect with historical and social issues. We are living in an era of great social upheaval. We have faced a global pandemic that has changed the way we work, business, public health, worship, and education. It has also exposed deeper national issues that we face with ever greater urgency. Our political system is mired in partisan rancor and controlled by the super wealthy. Systems of racism rob many African Americans of opportunities to forge a better life. Poverty's grip continues to tighten around the throats of millions of Americans. Our institutions are struggling to manage the pace of change and complex challenges we face while delivering services and goods to people. Technology simultaneously binds us together and serves as a tool tearing us apart.

We live in a time of questioning. We question what is true, what is false, and who can be trusted to discern which is which. Individual freedom and personal whim have trumped trusted sources of information and wisdom as people turn to anyone willing to confirm their suspicions and biases. In this moment, people are turning to and away from churches as they seek to understand all that is swirling around them. In this moment, we need to reimagine the Bible's relevance for today.

More and more people are asking hard and important questions about God, theology, faith, and the Bible. I, for one, believe the church needs people asking hard questions about these fundamental matters. Powerful forces in churches, however, are trying to shut down questions and conversations. One way they do this is by quoting a text in the Bible as if this verse is the one and only answer to complex historical and social issues. Nothing pains me more than hearing Christians arrogantly and ignorantly quote a Scripture to shut down questions and conversations about God, theology, faith, church, or the Christian life. I am distrubbed by the large number of people who think like this. Shutting people down by not listening and engaging questions and concerns is reckless and sometimes abusive. It is not pastoral because it does not express God's care for others. It is also not evangelistic. Shutting people down is one reason churches continue to lose people. Worse yet, relying on one quoted verse reflects a myopic ignorance of the Bible and Christian history, as if other verses cannot counter or she light on the quoted verse. It also ignores legitimate questions that come from experience, social realities, and important historical issues, and it has given rise to a shallow and bankrupt form of faith collapsing everywhere around us.

The theological issues we face today are too complex. It will not do to use the kind of selective proof-texting that allows some Christians to remarry and eat bacon while quoting Leviticus to condemn gay people. It is time to move beyond the weaponization of the Bible. It is time to avoid approaches that discourage dialogue about issues of faith. It is time to craft spaces in our minds and in our churches for a theological vision that is bigger than the small theologies that have for centuries propped up colonialism, racism, militarism, and capitalism. People are raising honest questions about concequential issues, things like eternal hell for "the lost"; why women cannot pastor churches in so many Christian traditions; and why American Christianity has failed so miserably to address slavery, racism, and poverty. Black people are asking why slave owners and racists get to go to heaven for being members of predominately white churches, while Africans are cursed to be slaves and experience hell on earth because of something Ham did to his father in Gen 9. Scores of Black people from the nineteenth century to today find it difficult accept that white Christianity is an authentic expression of the gospel of Jesus Christ. These issues are complex and require more than trite "well, the Bible says" responses. Some people know that the Bible says a range of things about these matters. What they want to know, what's driving them from God and our churches, is the meaning of the Bible for these issues. They want to know if problematic verses actually reflect the "core message" of the Bible in the first place. The emphasis on the core message of the Bible provides space to listen to questions and engage conversations about important matters of faith instead of shutting them down because they contradict a particular verse in Scripture. More importantly, the core message of the Bible provides space for people to disagree about many of these matters because the boundaries of faith are bigger than any one Christian, church, denomination, or creed.

We need an approach to interpretation that opens doors for questioning and provides opportunities for dialogue, not one that continues to shut them down because "the Bible is the word of God" and beyond questioning. Echoing the famous words of Karl Barth, we need to do theology with the Bible in one hand and the newspaper in the other. Today, we need a theology of biblical interpretation that holds the Bible in one hand but has a heart of compassion willing to listen to others. We need sound interpretive practices but also compassionate interpretative hearts and open interpretive ears.

When we learn to listen with care and discernment, we will find that questions are seeds that require the water of respect, dialogue, humility, and ambiguity. People are not turning away from God as much as they are turning away from bankrupt expressions of faith, many of which are based on problematic interpretations of the Bible. Our challenge is learning to use the Bible as a tool to deepen faith in God. Learning this will help us reimagine the Bible's relevance for today.

To do this, we have to abandon our fear. Too many churches allow fear to guide their engagement with culture and the issues we face today. Paul reminded Timothy that "God did not give us a spirit of fear, but of power, love, and a sound mind" (2 Tim 1:7). Fear paralyzes our ability to be appropriately responsive to the crises we face today. It also forces us into a defensive posture that is often unnecessary. This is what prevents us from listening and compels us to attack others because they are asking honest questions. The fear that they may be onto something and I could be wrong about an issue, or that there is more to God than they know, is a powerful deterrent to listening. We can claim all we want that we are defending God and biblical truth, but all we are doing is making it incredibly difficult for people to discover deeper and more authentic forms of faith.

There are Christians fighting to defend God and biblical truth when they don't have to. The gospel calls us to be witnesses, not warriors. Imagine what could happen if we shifted from the language of "fighting" for the faith to "giving witness" to the gospel of Jesus Christ. The implications are significant. It tamps down the need to be defensive or to attack people who do not share our belief system, and it invites us to share who God is to us and to listen to others as they share the same. Instead of using verses to prove that someone else is wrong, we share the ways God uses Scripture to guide, strengthen, inspire, and challenge us. The ways in which Scripture challenges us provide an opening to talk about problematic texts and the broader theological vision of the Bible, and the implications of these for life today. We have to be prepared to listen to people struggling with their faith and to people who have lost their faith. I have learned that God will allow us to lose faith. But I have also learned that this loss can be a path to a deeper faith. Often, the path to deeper expressions of faith begins by listening to people we were likely told to hate, marginalize, and categorize as evil. I know these things because they happened to me.

My Journey of Losing and Deepening Faith

There is a serious need to reframe how we think about the Bible, and an important aspect of this is reframing how we think about faith, especially losing one's faith. Losing one's faith is often taboo in the church. In my forty-nine years in church, I have not heard a sermon framing the loss of faith in a positive light. It always carries a negative connotation, often described as unbelief or giving into doubt. I have counseled Christians who felt faith was something they did not have enough of. They felt they always needed more faith to be a better Christian.

Sometimes "losing your faith" is described in dramatic terms like "hitting rock bottom," an experience that should be avoided at all costs, the end of a good and the beginning of a sad, lonely, and defeated chapter in life. That is why some preachers go to great lengths in sermons to admonish people, "whatever you do, don't lose your faith." If this message is true for church goers, we can imagine just how problematic it is for ministers to lose their faith. Some feel trapped by beliefs with which they struggle. Some feel pressured to toe the denominational line even if their beliefs have evolved in some ways that are no longer in concert with unquestioned beliefs of their church. Some ministers feel like frauds for preaching interpretations about which they have serious doubts or unresolved questions. In these cases, one cannot but help detect the undercurrent of fear that maybe they don't have enough faith or because they had lost it altogether.

Some of this fearfulness may be due to stories in the Gospels in which the disciples of Jesus gave into fear or did not exercise belief in a given situation. In one story, Jesus asks them, "where is your faith?" (Luke 8:25). In another story, Jesus tells a parable in which he says if one has faith the size of a mustard seed, one can move mountains (Matt 17:20). As helpful these stories are for some aspects of life, I think a real need exists to have a different kind of conversation about faith, one that encompasses the whole of one's life and faith as something one struggles with in a healthy manner.

New Testament stories abound of disciples and other people struggling with faith. These stories illustrate the ways God understands and responds to aspects of faith. For example, Peter denies Jesus, and yet it is Jesus who seeks him and encourages him to continue his journey of faith (John 21). Even then, Peter does not get everything right with his faith. Later God exposes and expands Peter's limited vision of faith with a dream and visit to a stranger's house (Acts 10). In Acts, God used experience to challenge and correct beliefs Peter held about Gentiles, an experience that caused a significant shift in his understanding of God and the world. New Testament writers often use language for faith that suggests it is path or a journey that one embarks on, grows to understand, and deepen. Paul speaks of humans having "a measure of faith" (see for instance, Rom 12:3), that faith is a fruit of the Spirit's work in a person's life (Gal 5:22), and that faith comes (think "grows") by hearing (think "understanding") the word of God (Rom 10:17). The epistle Peter speaks of the need to add to one's faith (2 Pet 1:5). This imagery and language is especially helpful because it challenges us to stop thinking of faith as a possession. Faith is so much more than what we have or do not have. It is more than a creed one says, a doctrine one believes, or a sermon one hears. In fact, I have found that faith is something we can lose, find, and deepen.

Many churches, but not all, reduce faith to accepting their teachings or creeds. Scripture teaches that faith is more than subscribing to certain beliefs. The language of "a measure of faith" in Rom 12 implies that faith is given to every person. The image of walking by faith in 2 Cor 5:7 implies that faith is a path. Language that faith comes from hearing the message and the need to add to your faith in Rom 10:17 and 2 Pet 1 implies that faith can grow. A faith that one lives out and grows in suggests that faith is more than beliefs tied to one's church. Faith is the way humans respond to God and God's work in the world. Faith is primarily relational, rooted in the call to love God and neighbor in the broadest sense of that word. It is propositional but in a secondary sense. Faith embraces certain beliefs, expresses itself in the form of beliefs, and responds to beliefs as one's understanding grows. Beliefs are dynamic, not static, reflections of one's faith. We often express our faith by what we believe, but it is important not to conflate the two. Faith is ultimately an expression of who we are and strive to be in response to God's work in the world and our lives. When understood this way, losing aspects of one's faith and its accompanying beliefs is inevitable and healthy.

I have lost "aspects" of my faith. Today, my faith does not resemble the faith I held to in earlier years of life and ministry. Certain core beliefs I still hold to: God as creator, the redemptive and saving work of Jesus Christ for humanity, the Bible as an authoritative source for faith, all humans are sinful, God's love for all humanity and desire for all to live in fellowship with them. Some beliefs I no longer hold, beliefs such as women cannot lead churches as pastors, that God will send people in same-gendered relationships to hell, that most people are going to hell and only a few people will be saved, that the Bible is inerrant and infallible, that God curses non-tithers even if they are relatively poor and can barely make a living, and that the saved will be raptured before a tribulation period that ends with Jesus slaughtering humans as the king of kings and lord of lords. These are beliefs I was taught by churches I attended and beliefs I advocated and defended as a pastor and minister.

Over the past fifteen years, I have learned that these beliefs are not only problematic but oppressive to women, to LGBTQ persons, people in other faith traditions, people congregations have hurt, and the poor who are mostly victims of exploitative and unjust systems and policies. Sometimes I feel shame that I advocated such beliefs—persecuting gay people, participating in frenzied moments of homophobia as preachers called for gay people to be delivered, and telling women they need to be submissive to men in the church and home. I have come to realize that these beliefs dehumanized and harmed people created and loved by God.

I have also amended certain beliefs I hold about God. For example, I have had to amend my belief that God "will step in and deliver us from trouble," one of the core beliefs of African American churches. The truth is that God does not intervene in the affairs of humans like we read in the Old Testament. The Israelites were freed from Egyptian slavery. Daniel was divinely protected in the lion's den and his friends in the furnace of fire, but Black people have been beaten, lynched, economically exploited, and killed in America for hundreds of years. A great number of people doing these evil things claim to be Christians. Eight Black Christians in Charleston, South Carolina, were murdered in a church while praying and were not protected by God. Native Americans are God's children, too. Native American sisters and brothers were victims of genocide and given no protection from God at the vicious hands of people claiming to be Christian. I cannot in good conscience continue to believe that God will step in and deliver us from trouble, much less preach and teach it. This does not mean God is not present and active in the world. God is present and at work in creation, just not in the immediate interventionist ways I was led to believe.

I have also found that God does not punish evil nations that oppress people. One cannot help but notice the absence of supernatural miracles directed against wicked empires like those we read about in Scripture—no floods, plagues, parting seas, fire from heaven, or angels killing armies. We do not see God doing things like this today, yet so many Christians believe these kinds of miracles can happen. There is no escaping the intellectual contradiction in believing in a God who does not change but seems to have on this issue. I am prompted to ask, "why miracles then and not now?" Trite claims that we see miracles every day do not satisfy.

Evil nations and rulers in government, the military, and business thrive in today's world and cause suffering beyond our ability to measure. Think of the hundreds of thousands of people in refugee camps because of wars and other military conflicts. Where is the divine intervention for them as they sleep in tents and barely survive? The country I live in has a dark history of genocide, slavery, wars, and mass incarceration. Yet, we don't see evidence that God has judged us for centuries of violence against untold millions of people. The God of Genesis and Exodus would not let America off the hook for its human rights atrocities. I admit I used to believe these things, but I no longer hold to them because they do not help me understand the world I live in now and what it means to live a faithful life to God.

I am not making this confession for shock value. This comes about after a long journey with God who has patiently opened my eyes to a deeper and healthier understanding of faith's power for life. Over the years, I have learned a few things about losing, finding, and deepening faith. It took me years to learn that beliefs can be held, relinquished, amended, and challenged without meaning I don't have faith. It is actually a sign of faith. First, I found that losing faith can be a way to connect with one's humanity and the ways religious sin warps our thinking and behavior. Second, I came to see that losing faith can be a sign of spiritual growth. Third, I realized that giving up certain beliefs did not destroy my faith. It actually deepened it and gave it a focus on things that really matter to me and others. For example, getting my eyes off miracles and moral minutia allowed me to give serious attention to the callous neglect and indifference churches have toward human suffering or the ways churches practice and justify hatred toward others, issues that affect billions of people on this planet.

There is a fourth and final lesson I will share. Losing and deepening my faith reflects my struggle in the church and with the church. I learned that it is OK to struggle with faith, and more importantly, one does not have to leave the church because of this struggle. There is room for us to struggle from within the broad confines of the church, though sometimes the church can feel anything but broad. I accept that not everyone will agree with me. I am fine with that. Last time I checked, I am not God, neither are those who disagree with me, and so disagreement does not have to define my struggle, though this tension is healthy as it provides some modicum of accountability and structure from which to think and argue theologically. In the end, losing aspects of my faith has been positive. It has enriched my life, deepened my faith, and helped me to become a better neighbor to others.

REIMAGINING THE BIBLE'S RELEVANCE FOR TODAY

Wrestling with Human Experience and Meaning

When I started taking seriously the experiences of people, both in history and today, my faith journey evolved most dramatically. One of the biggest problems I had as a young Christian was ignoring the struggles of others and their implications for God's work in the world. I would too easily hide behind verses in the Bible, using them as props that allowed me to ignore questions that experience raises about God, faith, and truth, and their intersection with the Bible. In time, I began to realize I was not honoring God fully because I gave little regard for the reality of others, especially those outside my church or social bubble. Not only was I not honoring God, but I was also not being faithful to the gospel of Jesus Christ. Why do I say this? John 3:16 says "for God so loved the world." This is a foundational verse and a core tenet of the gospel. It shows the very reason God sent his son Jesus into the world—deep abiding love for humanity. Taking God's love for the world and not just the people in my church or denomination has serious and significant implications for my faith and the faith of other Christians.

Doing this means affording *all* humans respect and love. It also implies the need for a general openness to others and a refusal to define them by my limited thinking and experiences. This is a way to live out another important aspect of the gospel. Jesus's call to discipleship in places like Mark 8 and Luke 9 require us to deny ourselves. This means our beginning point for a life of discipleship is not us but others.

Over the past decade and a half, I have learned to respect others by listening to their stories. It started when I began reading slave narratives. Africans were enslaved in America for more than 240 years. Many generations knew only the life of an enslaved person with little to no prospects of freedom. Reading their stories was one of the hardest experiences of my life. It changed me. When I was forced to exercise compassion by imagining life in this way, it began to change some of the questions about God and faith that I asked. I began with enslaved Africans but eventually had to grapple with the experiences of others—enslaved persons in history, Native Americans, and the poor, to name a few. Grappling with their quest for meaning in life has been one of the most difficult and important challenges to my faith. As I listened to them, I had to ask questions like, "Would I believe the same way I do now if I were a slave on a southern plantation in the 1800s or lived in a shantytown in South America?"

Grappling with the kind of faith these people had, despite a life with no prospect of freedom or a life mired in abject poverty, played a pivotal role in the deepening of my faith. More importantly, their experiences changed my questions, my theology, and my faith. I started asking questions like "What is my religion doing to alleviate and prevent mass human suffering today?" and "How are we using our moral influence, financial resources, and religious imaginations to curb widespread suffering and death?" I found the answers to these sorts of questions to be sourcs of great disappointment and moral challenge.

Compassion taught me an important truth about faith. Faith has to be responsive to lived realities and the questions that arise from them. Faith is not some static assent to beliefs. Formerly, I was taught to begin theology with Bible verses that were almost always taken out of context and used to give meaning and direction to life. When lived realities do not quite fit verses in Scripture, instead of interpreting those texts with care, I was told to conform my life to verses that had nothing to do with questions from a world more advanced than the world of the ancients or to verses coming from an entirely different cultural era than mine. This former approach is deeply problematic as it neither honors the biblical text nor does it appreciate the ways God's Spirit is at work in people's lives, ultimately and inevitably failing to abide by the gospel of Jesus Christ. Jesus encountered this wrongheaded approach to religion in his life. Religious leaders of his day cared more about rules and the letter of the law than the deeper intent and will of God for human thriving. Unlike them, Jesus sought to bring experience to bear on theological meaning, which has significant implications for faith.

What does this have to do with the Bible? If selective verses in the Bible are our beginning and end for theology and meaning instead of human experience, we will limit the kind of questions we raise and the answers we find. Sometimes God will use people's experiences to open up the text in ways previously hidden to us. When I started listening and showing compassion for others, it changed what I saw when I read the Bible. When I saw differently, my theology about the Bible changed in meaningful ways. Not ignoring human experience was absolutely essential in the evolution of my faith, both its loss and eventual deepening.

It is only fitting to end a book about approaching problematic texts in the Bible with a discussion of faith. My attempts here are not to be sensational but pastoral in a way that helps us reimagine the Bible's relevance in an age of questioning, change, and challenge for churches. I hope my readers know that questioning texts in the Bible does not have to end in disbelief. God can actually use questioning to deepen faith and provide paths for the revitalization that American Christianity so desperately needs. Ultimately, the Bible should help people make sense of human experience, history, and the social systems that give meaning to life. Giving careful attention to problematic texts, while discerning the core message of the Bible, gives us ways to reimagine the Bible's relevance for today. This book is a product of my endeavor to do this in a way that respects the integrity of experience. The gospel requires us to love God and neighbor, and ultimately to lift up the mysterious workings of God in and through Scripture that nurtures and deepens faith.

Afterword

A Pastoral and Theological Response

I HAVE FOUND DR. Brogdon's work to be both helpful and refreshing. As a pastor, I am responsible for assisting my congregation in developing a love for Scripture and an ability to interpret it well. Unfortunately, many of the resources available tend to emphasize either pure devotion or an exclusively critical lens. Being able to offer them an approach that is both reverent and critical is extremely valuable. Assuring believers that "faith and intellectual honesty can work together" is an important component of pastoral care. My own calling has been affirmed and enriched by the scholarship and friendship of Lewis Brogdon.

Quite honestly, I owe my vocational identity and love of scripture in large part to Dr. Brogdon's friendship and guidance. As I began studies at Louisville Seminary, I had many unresolved questions about ministry and the Bible. My primary concern was in how the "Good Book" had been used to justify terrorism against enslaved Africans and the continued abuse of oppressed communities. I had attempted to forsake the reading of scripture altogether, but I desperately wanted to recover the sense of truth and grace I had originally found in the Bible.

About halfway through my degree program, I enrolled in an African American Hermeneutics course taught by Dr. Brogdon. It was an evening class, which gave us the opportunity to sit for hours at a time discussing how African Americans, from the days of slavery up to the present, have interpreted Scripture. As I stretched my mind to grasp the complexity and simplicity of various heuristics, my entire way of dealing with scripture began to change. I began to understand that most Americans have privileged a set of hermeneutical principles that were developed primarily by those in power. Whether it was viewing scripture as a preserver of the status quo or as a corroboration of one group's superior status, these broad themes were used to both explain and ignore particular aspects of the sacred text. Yet, interestingly enough, much of the Bible was written by those who did not hold much, if any, political or social power. Large parts of the Hebrew Bible were written in exile and the lion's share of the New Testament was recorded by those who practiced an illegal religion. The Bible is the product of God communication through oppressed people. So, in our attempts to interpret Scripture well, Dr. Brogdon taught us to pay attention to the hermeneutics of other oppressed people. This unlocked something inside me.

For years, I had drawn deep inspiration from and developed meaningful relationships with people of color. My faith had been particularly enriched by experienced within African American congregations. Indeed, my family's own Pentecostal tradition owes its very existence to the influence of various streams of Black Christianity. When I became more reflective about this, I recognized that the faith of African Americans was, and is, informed by a unique hermeneutical habit: "Holding problematic passages in tension with the core theological message(s) of the text." Adopting this habit in my approach to scripture has propelled me beyond the impasse set by the problematic texts in question.

I could not be a preacher if I had to choose between intellectual honesty and an understanding of the Bible as God's word. Thankfully, Dr. Brogdon has helped me and many others (not just preachers!) navigate the minefield of biblical interpretation and discern the truth of God's love and grace. As he writes near the end of this book, "Truth has to be incarnational—eternal and worldly, perfect and imperfect." Scripture is messy, but with the guidance of the Holy Spirit and wise teachers like Lewis Brogdon, we can discover its beauty and wisdom once again.

Rev. Beau Brown, Indianapolis, Indiana

Bibliography

"The 14 Most Abominable Bible Verses." http://www.news24.com/MyNews24/ The-14-Most-Abominable-Bible-Verses-20121224.

Alexander, Estrelda. "Political Theology and Hermeneutics." Classroom lecture notes, RTCH 720-Contemporary Theologies, Spring 2008, typed notes.

Augustine. *The Confessions of Saint Augustine.* Translated by Rex Warner. New York: Penguin Putnam, 1963.

Bailey, Randall C. *Yet With a Steady Beat: Contemporary U. S. Afrocentric Biblical Interpretation.* Atlanta: Society of Biblical Literature, 2003.

Bal, Mieke. *Anti-Covenant: Counter-Reading Women's Lives in the Hebrew Bible.* JSOTSup 81: Sheffield: Almond, 1989.

Brogdon, Lewis. *A Companion to Philemon.* Foreord by Marion Soards. Cascade Companions. Eugene, OR: Cascade, 2018

Brown, Michael Joseph. *The Blackening of the Bible: The Aims of African American Biblical Scholarship.* New York: Trinity, 2004.

Brown, Raymond. *Introduction to the New Testament.* New York: Doubleday, 1997.

Callahan, Allen Dwight. *The Talking Book.* New Haven, CT: Yale University Press, 2006.

Collins, John. *Does the Bible Justify Violence?* Minneapolis: Fortress, 2004.

Douglass, Frederick. "Writings." In *Slaves in the New Testament,* edited by J. Albert Harrill, 177. Minneapolis: Fortress, 2006.

Elliot, E. N. *Cotton is King.* New York: Negro Universities Press, 1969.

Felder, Cain Hope. *Stony the Road We Trod.* Minneapolis: Fortress, 1991.

Gibson, David. "We Revere the Bible . . . We Don't Read It." *The Washington Post,* December 9, 2020. https://www.washingtonpost.com/archive/ local/2000/12/09/we-revere-the-bible-we-dont-read-it/ff4d2cfd-7861- 44a0-ae59-d8bcdb4f2809/.

Hayes, John H. *Introduction to the Bible.* Philadelphia: Westminster, 1971.

Hughes, Allen, and Albert Hughes, dir. *The Book of Eli.* Burbank, CA: Warner Bros., 2010.

Kerrigan, Michael. *Dark History of the Bible.* London: Amber, 2015.

Kovacs, Joe. *Shocked by the Bible.* Nashville: W. Publishing Group,2008.

Loveday, Simon. *The Bible for Grownups.* London: Icon, 2016.

MacCammon, Linda M. *Liberating the Bible.* New York: Orbis, 2008.

Myers, Jeremy. "11 Bible Verses That Turn Christians Into Atheists." https://www.patheos.com/blogs/unfundamentalistchristians/2016/04/11-bible-verses-that-turn-christians-into-atheists/.

Origen. "On First Principles, 2:9." In *Origen, An Exhortation to Martyrdom, Prayer and Selected Works,* edited by Rowan A. Greer, 175–88. New York: Paulist, 1979.

Parker, Angela. *If God Still Breathes, Why Can't I? Black Lives Matter and Biblical Authority.* Grand Rapids: Eerdmans, 2021.

Prothero, Stephen. *Religious Literacy.* New York: Harper One, 2007.

Spong, John Shelby. *The Sins of Scripture.* San Francisco: Harper Collins, 2005.

Stringfellow, Thorton. "The Bible Argument or Slavery in the Light of Divine Revelation." In *Cotton is King,* edited by E. N. Elliot, 461–92. New York: Negro Universities Press, 1969.

Swartley, William. *Slavery, Sabbath, War, and Women.* Scottdale, PA: Herald, 1983.

Thiselton, Anthony. *New Horizons in Hermeneutics.* Grand Rapids: Zondervan, 1992.

Thomas, Stacey Floyd, et al., eds. *Black Biblical Studies or Hermeneutics in Black Church Studies: An Introduction.* Nashville: Abingdon, 2007.

Thurman, Howard. *Jesus and the Disinherited.* Boston: Beacon, 1976.

Torrey, R. A. *Difficulties in the Bible.* New Kensington, PA: Whitaker House, 1996.

Trible, Phyllis. *Texts of Terror.* Philadelphia: Fortress, 1984.

Wimbush, Vincent. *The Bible and African Americans.* Minneapolis: Fortress, 2003.